Streams
That
Make
Glad

Charles Elliott Newbold, Jr.

Front cover photograph, titled *Tranquility*, was taken by Deryck Coetzer in South Africa on the Mooiriver (translated "beautiful river") on a farm called The Bend. www.deryckphotoworld.com.

For additional reading see: www.charlesnewbold.com

The chapters within this volume are pastoral articles that were first published by permission in *Validity Magazine*, Hohenwald, Tennessee, USA, between October 2011 and February 2015. Found online at: validitymag.com

Thank you, Becky Jane and Charles Elliott (Shane) Newbold, III, for the privilege of contributing these articles to *Validity Magazine*.

Thanks to my wife, Nancy, who as chief editor of all my writings makes them reader friendly.

"There is a river, the streams whereof shall make glad the city of God, the holy place of the tabernacles of the most High." Psalm 46:4.

CONTENTS

Be Found in Christ 1

Unto Him 4

The Measuring Stick of Criticism 6

Intimacy with the Lord 9

Fruit-Bearing Fig Trees 12

The Real End times: Should I be Afraid? 15

Sir, We Would See Jesus 18

What God Wants 21

What Are You Into? 24

Living As Sons 27

Patience, Please 30

Liberty in Forgiveness 33

Maturity 36

Try Jesus 39

Dashed Hopes 42

Reforming Old Systems 45

Genie in a Bottle 48

Revival or Revolution 51

Jesus Plus Nothing 54

Who Does Your Life Say That I Am? 57

The Finished Work of God 60

Whose Are you? 63

Finishing Well 66

Dare to be light 69

Duh! 72

Free Trip to Heaven: Inquire Within 75

Tapestry 78

Impossible Resolutions 81

Velvety Soft Cheek 84

Fruit of the Spirit 87

The Life of the Tree 90

In Whom We Believe 93

Setting the Tone in the Home 96

Love Is a Choice 99

Old Dogs and New Tricks 102

Following Jesus 105

America Bless God 108

Give Thanks with a Grateful Heart 111

A Hug from Jesus 114

I Love Knowing… 117

BE FOUND IN CHRIST

As foreign as it may sound, our goal as Christians is not our salvation, godliness, holiness, and righteousness. It certainly is not to get saved so we will miss hell and go to heaven. These are byproducts of putting our trust in Jesus Christ. Rather, our goal should be only this: to "be found in Him." Philippians 3:8-11.

As we are found in Him, we find: (1) that salvation comes to us, we do not have to pursue it; (2) that salvation, godliness, holiness, and righteousness comes to us, we do not have to pursue them; (3) that all the blessings of God pursue us, we do not have to pursue them. We set our affection upon Him, not upon the attaining to anything for ourselves. "Let this mind be in you…" Philippians 2:5.

The most difficult mindset of religion is to realize that the gospel is not the good news of man, but the good news of God. It has all to do with what God wants, not what we want.

Now we all agree that God wants us "saved." The trouble, however, is that men are deceived by their own self-centeredness into pursuing salvation for their own sakes. We are to pursue the Savior—pursue Him for His sake. Pursue Him because He is worthy of the sacrifice of our lives. We pursue Him to honor Him, to worship Him, to praise Him and to be a people of praise for Him. Everything we do is for Him. We give no thought for ourselves. Such loss of life for His sake is the only means by which God has ordered for us to find life. Even then, the life we find is not our own, but His. "Be found in Him." Philippians 3:9a. "For you died, and your life is hidden with Christ in God." Colossians 3:3.

What God wants, even intends to do is to bring us to the end of ourselves. Any so-called gospel that centers upon man or that which is attained for self is perverted and false. The gospel of God—that is, the good news of the Kingdom—is God. It is God centered. It has to do with what He wants and it should be our life's ambition to give God what He wants. He is the Savior and our salvation; He is our justifier and our justification; He is our deliverer and our deliverance; He is the sanctifier and our sanctification; He is the glorifier and our glorification. It has all to do with who He is, not what we are or ever hope to be.

Nevertheless, as we are found in Him and He is found in us, we find our true identity. Our true identity is not again who we are, but who He is. We are who He is in us. This is a very difficult concept to grasp since we are so earthly minded. Nevertheless, God wants to bring us to a place in Him where our focus is no longer upon ourselves or upon the outward nature of things, but upon Him and His kingdom within.

We are not building for ourselves. We build for Him. We

build by Him—by His power only. We build according to Him. We build what He wants built: namely, His spiritual house, not what we imagine He wants.

The good news is God loves us, wants us, and has made a way for us to come to Him. The fact is, He made a way for Himself to come to us. That way is Jesus, the Messiah of God and the blood atonement of the Lamb of God. The good news is all bundled up into who Jesus is and what He did. He died for us while we were yet sinners. Romans 5:8. He finished God's work of redemption on the cross. It is by His grace we are saved through faith in Him. Ephesians 2:8. But we are "saved" for Him. The wondrous by-product of being saved for God is that salvation then comes to us. That is good news indeed.

Yet, the paradox: He who is found in true existence is found in God, fulfilling the will of God at all loss to our own self will. Be found in Him. Surrender your will to the absolute will of the Father of lights and you will find Him. He is waiting.

2

UNTO HIM

Notice the progression of the following questions, how they begin with "me" and end with God.

What do I want to do today?

What do I want God to do today?

What does God want me to do today?

What does God want to do through me today?

What does God want to do today?

What is God doing today?

We need to move away from a ME perspective to a God perspective, from an earthly view to a heavenly view.

We have to ask the right question to get to the right answer.

Once we understand what God is doing, we will have a better idea of our part in it; but we must remember, it is not what we are doing or ever could do for God. It is all about what God is doing for Himself in and through us. We do not live our lives unto ourselves, nor does God exist to live His life unto us. We live our lives unto Him, unto His ultimate purposes and intentions. DeVern Fromke in his book titled *The Ultimate Intention* wrote, "[People] are more alive to what they want God to do for them than what they might become unto Him."

This is what Jesus meant when He said, "If any man desires to come after Me, let him deny himself, and take up his cross, and follow Me." Matthew 16:24. That is to say, we simply live our lives unto Him and no longer for Self.

This sacrificial living is the highest worship—the highest sacrifice of praise we can offer unto Him. This is heart, soul, and strength service and not merely lip service. You cannot program this sort of praise and worship.

God, through His Holy Spirit, is looking for, even releasing a people in the earth today who will truly worship Him in spirit and truth, who will truly make that sacrifice of praise unto Him.

This worship is a sweet smelling aroma that rises to heaven and is pleasing to the nostrils of God.

When God does move on our behalf, as He surely will, we want to recognize it, receive it, and joyfully thank Him for it. Nevertheless, we do nothing for God in order to get from God.

The challenge of the day, of every day is to discern what God is doing and put our hands to that.

3

THE MEASURING STICK OF CRITICISM

Have you ever wondered why we suffer some of the things we do? Health issues? Emotional anguishes? Financial woes? Relationship problems?

Many of our problems are the obvious result of such things as overeating, over-spending, over-drinking, over-smoking, over-doing it, and physical inactivity. Good self-help programs exist that can help us deal with many of these problems when self-discipline seems to fail us.

There is one cause of suffering we never think about. It may be the culprit behind more of our problems than we want to admit. It is called criticism.

Jesus said that it is not what goes into the mouth that defiles a man, but what comes out. Matthew 15:11. Press the pause button here for a moment and think about what kinds of words spew out of your mouth. James wrote that out of the mouth comes both blessing and cursing, though this ought not to be the case. James 3:10. Then, there is that troubling principle Jesus warned about in Matthew 7:1-2. "Judge not, that you be not judged. For with what judgment you judge, you will be judged; and with the measure you use, it will be measured back to you." Lord have mercy on us! Criticism is a form of being judgmental.

"But I don't think I judge others," we might think. Even if we are not given to criticism, there are more subtle ways we judge others. We judge others whenever we think we are better than they. Perhaps we think we are better than they because we make more money, we are of a certain ethnic or racial group (as if we had anything to do about that choice), we belong to the right club, we go to the right church, or we have the right politics.

When we are critical or judgmental of another, we set ourselves up as a judge over them. We hold up a measuring stick and declare that they do not measure up.

But here is the "gotcha!" We are the ones holding up that measuring stick, right? That means we are standing right next to it. That means the stick by which we measure others is measuring us as well. Chances are we will not measure up to our own standard.

Moreover, we will likely be tested to see if we measure up. Critically judging others will in itself put us on the short end of that stick. The criticisms and judgments we make of others boomerang on us; hence, we unnecessarily bring trouble upon ourselves.

What's the solution? First off, we humble ourselves and repent. Admit the truth. Then, stop criticizing. Stop making judgments.

Secondly, pray for God to "deliver us from this evil."

Thirdly, our conscience may demand we seek forgiveness. We begin by asking for God's forgiveness. Then, we forgive ourselves. The hardest part is to go to that person we criticized and confess our violation to them, asking for their forgiveness. We do not just say, "I'm sorry." They already know that. They do not have to respond to that. But when you say, "Forgive, me," they have to respond one way or the other. At least we will have done our part.

Fourthly, every time we catch ourselves criticizing, we repeat steps one through three. The more we have to ask forgiveness, the more likely we are to stop the craziness. "Resist the devil and he will flee from you." James 4:7.

4

INTIMACY WITH THE LORD

Think about the people you know. You know some of them better than others. The spectrum goes from casual to intimate. "Oh, yeah, I heard about him, but I've never met him." "I shook hands with the Governor once." "I've read a lot about her and I feel as though I know her." "After forty years of marriage, we really do know each other."

Knowing about someone is different from knowing him or her. Intimacy has to do with sincerely knowing someone because we have shared life together at a deeper level — one that is open, honest, genuine, and sincere — a kind of closeness that is hard to describe.

Where then, on this spectrum would you put your relationship with the Lord Jesus Christ? Do you only know about Him from having studied your Bible? Or do you truly know Him because you are coupled in a personal relationship with Him.

He desires that we know Him and not just know about Him. He wants that one-on-one relationship as best of friends forever.

How, then, do we get to that place of intimacy with him? It begins by sharing the same kind of life that He has. Jesus told Nicodemus that he must be born again. John 3:7. Notice He said, "must" because there is no other way to eternal life. We must be born by His Holy Spirit from above. When we are born again, we receive His kind of life — eternal life. Jesus is eternal life; therefore, when we receive Jesus, we receive eternal life. We become a new creature — a new creation. 2 Corinthians 5:17. We become His kind of life. We have the same kind of nature as He. And this makes us sons of God. Romans 8:14. These are not figures of speech. This is a reality.

This divine sonship through the rebirth experience is accomplished by faith. Grace through faith. Ephesians 2:8. We come to really believe that He is the Son of God and that He died for us that we might be saved through Him. When we believe in such a way, He grants us His grace and we are born again. He made it simple.

This makes us His brothers. We have the same Father. Again, I say, this is not just a figure of speech. It is reality. Believe it!

Brothers talk. Brothers hang out. Brothers know each other. Brothers forgive. Brothers stand up for each other. Brothers reveal the secrets of their hearts. These are the kinds of things that make for an honest, dynamic, and intimate relationship.

Still, we need help getting to that place of intimacy with the Lord. He already knows us, but we need to come to know Him. The more we hang out with Him, the more we will surely get to know Him, His heart, His will, and His ways.

Nothing within ourselves can make this relationship possible. We need help. Because of His love for us and His desire for us to know Him, He has given us His Holy Spirit. We appeal to Him to immerse, soak, saturate, and baptize us in His precious Holy Spirit. The Holy Spirit is the source that powers that relationship.

He thirsts for that intimate relationship with us. He wants us to love Him with all of our heart, soul, mind, and strength. He does not want religion from us. He wants relationship.

Sure, it's important that we get our doctrines right, that we know the Bible, and that we pray and do good, but His deepest yearning is for us to truly know Him.

5

FRUIT-BEARING FIG TREES

It would seem that James, the brother of Jesus, opened up a can of worms when he wrote, "But someone will say, 'You have faith, and I have works.' 'Show me your faith without your works, and I will show you my faith by my works.'" Again he wrote, "...faith without works is dead" James 2:18,20.

That can is still open and the issue is still in contention two thousand years later. Whole denominations of churches are camped around one side of this issue or the other. One side believes that all we need is faith, that God's grace will cover our sins and weaknesses. The other side believes we need to add works to our faith, accusing the former side of "cheap grace," or an "easy believism," — that we can go on sinning as long as we believe.

What is the deal here? Are we saved by faith, by our works, or some combination of the two?

For James, it was neither faith without works nor works without faith, but a meshing of the two. The question is: which of these comes first? Does faith produce works or works produce faith? Can our works by any means save us? Neither side can win this debate. Scriptures support both. But, what if we have misunderstood this argument altogether?

James 3:12 asks, "Can the fig tree, my brethren, bear olives? Or a grape vine bear figs?" That explains it! Remember the time Jesus passed a fig tree and cursed it because it did not have any figs on it? Mark 11:20-21. What good is a fig tree if it does not bear figs? Jesus was not mad at the tree. He wanted to make a point. Everything He said and did was intended to make a point. So, what is the point that James is making?

Let's say the fig tree is faith and the figs are the works. When we put our trust in God's finished works in Christ, God grants us righteousness just as He did with Abraham. Abraham did not earn righteousness by his good works. He believed God and subsequently obeyed God. This obedience was his works. Faith produces righteousness and righteousness produces works. If you truly have faith, you will surely produce the works.

A grapevine cannot just decide, "I want to be a fig tree, so I will try to produce figs. Maybe if I can produce enough figs, I will become a fig tree." Not if you are a grapevine! But if the tree really is a fig tree, then it is bound to produce figs, unless it is dead. "Thus also faith by itself, if it does not have works, is dead." James. 2:17.

If we are righteous, then we will produce righteousness. Righteousness is the result of who we have been made to be by our faith in Christ. Our works could never save us. Never!

We cannot do righteous deeds in order to become righteous. We do righteous deeds because we are righteous.

Forget about trying to work your way into heaven. It will

not work. Rather, put your trust in the finished works of God in Christ and allow Him to turn you into a fig tree, bearing the fruit of righteousness.

"Now may the God of peace who brought up our Lord Jesus from the dead, that great Shepherd of the sheep, through the blood of the everlasting covenant, make you complete in every good work to do His will, working in you what is well pleasing in His sight, through Jesus Christ, to whom be glory forever and ever. Amen." Hebrews 13:20-21.

6

THE REAL END TIMES: SHOULD I BE AFRAID?

A lot of speculation is heard these days about the End Times. Some people believe that Jesus Christ is coming again soon and that this will be the end of the world. Some people saw further evidence of this possibility in the Mayan calendar that ended December 21, 2012; the unproven prophecies of Nostradamus; or in certain alignments in the solar system.

Jesus listed a number of things that are to happen before the end comes—false christs, nations rising against nations, earthquakes, famines, pestilences, persecution and betrayal. Luke 21. Generations before us have seen these events in their own time and thought it was The End. Obviously, it was not! While these signs have happened periodically throughout recorded history, they are occurring more frequently and with greater intensity.

The End-Time scenario pendulum swings from one extreme to the other. Religious groups fall out with each other over these different ideologies as if these were absolute doctrines of the gospel. Many believe that this end of the age will be preceded by God's judgment and by a period of great tribulation. Many believe they will be raptured out during the tribulation.

Such musings do one of two things in us. They either plunge us into the depths of fear or give rise to joyful anticipation, depending on what side of the fence you stand. Jesus said, "And when these things begin to come to pass, then look up, and lift up your heads; for your redemption draws near." Luke 21:28.

A terrified woman read me a paper she had prepared predicting these pending horrors. She was considering moving to the mountains to attempt a self-sufficient life. Many people are seeking such refuge.

I talked with her about the need to trust the Lord in all things, regardless of our circumstances.

I shared my personal convictions. "Because I have surrendered my life to Jesus, I am able to live my life knowing that I am no longer my own. Jesus purchased me with His precious shed blood when He died on the cross. I have been bought with a price. I am not my own. I belong to Him. Nothing can happen to me unless He says so. Whatever happens is His business, not mine." Paul the apostle wrote, "For if we live, we live to the Lord; and if we die, we die to the Lord. Therefore, whether we live or die, we are the Lord's." Romans 14:8. "For to me, to live is Christ, and to die is gain." Philippians 1:21.

I sensed within myself a serene disconnect from the world as I spoke these things. Even if these things happen in our time—and I am one who thinks they just might—I feel removed from them. I realize, of course, that we can never know for sure how we will face adversity until we actually face it.

Nevertheless, I felt a peace that had to be the work of the Lord in me. He desires to bring us to that place of rest in Him. After all, "the kingdom of God is not eating and drinking, but righteousness and peace and joy in the Holy Spirit." Romans 14:17.

This peace that passes all understanding settles upon us when King Jesus reigns and rules in our hearts and lives. When He rules, nothing else does. Come what may, there is nothing to fear.

7

SIR, WE WOULD SEE JESUS

Remember those Greeks in the New Testament who came to Philip one day and said, "Sir, we would see Jesus"? Considering all the miracles Jesus had performed and all the profound teachings He gave, who would not want to see this stranger from Galilee? He caused quite a stir. There were times that the crowd pressed Him so that He had to retreat to the mountains. So, it seems a bit bold of these guys to request a private sitting with Him.

Nevertheless, Philip and Andrew went together to tell Jesus about the request. He responded saying, "...Unless a grain of wheat falls into the ground and dies, it remains alone; but if it dies, it produces much grain. John 12:20-24.

What kind of a response was that? What does that have to do with them wanting to see Jesus?

For sure, they wanted to personally see this Jesus in His humanity. Perhaps they wanted to interview Him.

If you were granted that privilege, what might you ask Him? "Are you the Son of God?" "Are you the King of the Jews?" "Were you really born of a virgin?" "Do you really talk to God?" "What is that like?"

You could ask these kinds of questions, but where would that leave you? Jesus was obviously not interested in this kind of interview. Equally so, I am sure they were not interested in His knowledge of agriculture.

It even seems as if Jesus was answering a question they did not ask. So, what did Jesus mean by this strange response? As mysterious as it may appear on the surface, Jesus really was answering their question.

By using this illustration He was saying, "If you really want to see Me, you have to die." He was not suggesting they had to die and go to heaven before they would see Him. They had to die to self in their lifetime before they could really see Him. The same is true with us.

If we want to see Jesus; that is, to really know Him, we have to be as that grain of wheat and fall to the ground and die. We can try to get to know Him in the natural, physical sense, or we can know Him in the heavenly, spiritual sense. Which do you suppose is the better way?

"How do I die? Can I kill myself?" No! It is a death to self, but it could never be a self-inflicted death.

Jesus explained, "He who loves his life will lose it, and he who hates his life in this world will keep it for eternal life. If anyone serves Me, let him follow Me; and where I am, there My servant will be also. If anyone serves Me, him My Father will honor." John 12:25-26.

Once Jesus truly becomes the only thing that matters in our lives, we will no longer be interested in living for ourselves. We will desire Him to live His life through us.

Therefore, if you truly want to see Jesus, die! Die to your

old destructive, egocentric man of sin and death! Then, you will know Him in His resurrection, having been raised to newness of life in Him. Romans 6: 4.

"I have been crucified with Christ; it is no longer I who live, but Christ lives in me; and the life which I now live in the flesh I live by faith in the Son of God, who loved me and gave Himself for me." Galatians 2:20.

8

WHAT GOD WANTS

Have you ever thought about what God may want for Himself out of this deal between Him and us? Have you ever thought that it may not be all about us?

After all, He is the Creator. He is the one who set it all in motion. He must have had some purpose in mind — something He planned for Himself.

If you build model airplanes as a hobby, for whom would you be doing that, for the models or for yourself? "No brainer!" You would be doing it for your own pleasure.

Of course, God made us more dynamic and response-able than a model airplane, but the analogy does not fly far from comparison.

What if, just what if God made us for His pleasure alone? That would be a novel concept because we think God exists for us, for our good pleasure. He desires for us to take pleasure in Him, but not to use Him for our pleasure as if somehow we invented Him.

For the most part we have made God up to be the way we

want Him to be. We are more comfortable with Him being the god of our own making. I'm not really sure we would be comfortable with knowing what He really wants from us because it would no longer have to do with us. God wants more than for us to "get saved" so we can miss hell and go to heaven when we die.

What, then, does God want out of this deal with us?

DeVern Fromke in his book, *The Ultimate Intention*, summarized God's plan superbly: "The Father receives a vast family of sons like the First Born [Jesus]. The Son [Jesus] receives a glorious Body [Believers] for His expression. The Holy Spirit receives a temple of living stones for His eternal abode. The three in one receiving honor, glory, and satisfaction."

Colossians 1:16 instructs us that all things were created for Him. Revelation 4:11 adds that He has created all things for His pleasure. Hebrews 2:10 concludes, "For it became Him, for whom are all things, and by whom are all things, in bringing many sons unto glory, to make the captain of their salvation perfect through sufferings." Ephesians 4:13,15 speaks of our destiny saying, "...till we all come to the unity of the faith and of the knowledge of the Son of God, to a perfect man, to the measure of the stature of the fullness of Christ;...that we may grow up in all things into Him who is the head—Christ..." And my favorite: Galatians 4:19 "...until Christ is formed in you."

God intends to have a people of His own making—many sons who will show forth His glory in righteousness and holiness.

That is His intention and our destiny. We were created for that. How much more joy, peace, and satisfaction will be ours once we yield to what God wants and stop trying to exploit Him for what we want!

That is called surrender—surrendering our wills for His will. It is called the exchanged life. We would do well if we quit trying to live our self-absorbed, self-defeating lives and allow God in Christ through His Holy Spirit to live His liberating life in and through us.

Do you desire for God to have what He wants and intends? Tell Him in all sincerity, "Lord, I surrender my will and my ways to you. I want what you want at all cost to Self. Clearly reveal your will to me that I may walk in it daily."

9

WHAT ARE YOU INTO?

Toward the end of our long drive from Tennessee to western New York to visit our friends Bill and Marge, I thought about a question I wanted to ask Bill. I admit that it was a trick question with a right and wrong answer.

After our hellos and hugs, Bill grabbed some luggage and started up their steps in front of me. That was my moment.

"What have you been into lately?" I schemed.

It only took him a nanosecond to answer, "Jesus."

"Right answer!" I expected no less from him since I had known of his "in-the-garden" walk with the Lord for many years.

Think about this question for yourself. How would you have answered, not knowing it was a trick question?

"I'm really into fishing lately," might be your response. "Just into my career." "Right now my grandkids." "Gardening." "Crafts." "Gourmet cooking." "The playoffs on TV." "Golf." "Politics." "Reading novels." "Gold." Or, "Simply surviving." Then, there are those more noble sounding things like, "Church." "My ministry." "My club." Inasmuch as we are egomaniacs, we are mostly into ourselves.

There are as many different answers as there are people. These answers are quite normal and not to be taken as condemnation, unless of course we are into some bad stuff—drugs, boozing, gambling.

I'm not sure how I would have answered had I been caught off guard by this question. That is what makes it a trick question, asked only to make a point.

By asking this question, I mean to call attention to our priorities—those kinds of things that completely absorb us, almost to the degree of being lost in them.

Jesus proclaimed in Matthew 6:21 that "...where your treasure is, there will your heart be also." He said this in the context of laying up heavenly treasures rather than earthly treasures. We normally think this has to do with money, but not necessarily. Consider all the other things we treasure—those things that we are into. Consider the minefield of distractions that divert our attention away from that simplicity and purity of devotion to Jesus—so many different things we can be into and with little thought about how much those things have gotten into us.

"Hey, Jesus, what are you into these days?" We actually know His answer from His statement in John 5:19, "...the Son can do nothing of Himself, but what He sees the Father do; for whatever He does, the Son also does in like manner." I would say Jesus was into the Father, doing the Father's business.

One might say, "Yeah, but that was Jesus." Maybe so! Nevertheless, Hebrews exhorts, "Therefore, holy brethren, partakers of the heavenly calling, consider the Apostle and

High Priest of our confession, Christ Jesus,." Hebrews 3:1. The word, "consider," means, "to consider attentively, fix one's eyes or mind upon...."

Hebrews 12:1-2 reads, "Therefore we also, since we are surrounded by so great a cloud of witnesses, let us lay aside every weight, and the sin which so easily ensnares us, and let us run with endurance the race that is set before us, looking unto Jesus, the author and finisher of our faith, who for the joy that was set before Him endured the cross, despising the shame, and has sat down at the right hand of the throne of God."

We desire for Jesus to be the focal point of our lives. We treasure Him and Him alone. Therefore, should someone ask you, "What are you into?" I pray you will be able to matter-of-factly and boldly answer, "Jesus!"

10

LIVING AS SONS

We hear it preached that we are the sons of God, but it always seems like a figure of speech. Well, it is not! If we are truly born-again believers in Jesus, we are the living and breathing sons of God, male or female. The Holy Spirit made us sons. We have His DNA (Divine Nature Attributes). Almighty God created us for Himself from the beginning with the intent of having many sons, according to the patterned Son, Jesus Christ. This is our calling, our destiny. He chose us to be His sons — sons of the living God. Imagine that!

Consider the privilege and honor of being sons of the living God. As such, we are co-inheritors with His Son, Jesus Christ. Romans 8:17. He is the Son of God and we are the sons of God. We have a shared interest in all that pertains to His kingdom. We are sons of the kingdom of God. God reigns and rules through His only begotten Son, Jesus Christ, who is the King of God's kingdom. Jesus is the King of kings, Lord of lords, Prince of peace, Almighty God, and Everlasting Father.

I drive this point home because most of us who have believed upon the name of Jesus have not comprehended the greatness and magnitude of living as sons of the living God. We simply have not known who we are. As a consequence, many believers are living defeated and powerless lives. Many allow the enemy of their soul to play havoc in their lives, not knowing that we have authority to overcome.

The greatest enemy we face is that Garden-of-Eden pride that rises up within us, causing us to think that we are the captains of our souls—the governors of our destinies, that we can have life the way we want it.

We can attempt to live life the way we want it because God has given us incredible free will. Free will is necessary. While He commanded us to love Him with all of our hearts, souls, minds, and strengths, it has to be our choice to do so. Love has to be a choice in order for it to be genuine. Love cannot be legislated.

Left to our own devices, we love ourselves more than God—more than anything. This has to change. If we so choose to love God with all of our hearts, souls, minds, and strengths, then we are destined to be His sons and to reap the harvest that comes with being sons of His Kingdom.

Remember the prodigal son story in the Bible? Though he was a son, he chose of his own free will to leave the protection and provision of His father's domain. The father released him to go his own way. The wayward son squandered his life. Most people live squandered lives because they do not appreciate their birthright as sons in God's glorious kingdom. They do not live as sons. Even the older brother, who did not leave his father, failed to fully appreciate who he was and what rightfully belonged to him. Luke 15:11-32.

Hear, now, the call of your heavenly Father today. Repent

(turn) from thinking you are your own god. Rejoice in the meek and humble knowledge that, if we so choose to live as such, we are sons of the living God. The inheritance is ours here and now.

"Behold what manner of love the Father has bestowed on us, that we should be called children of God!." 1 John 3:1.

11

PATIENCE, PLEASE

Have you ever heard it jokingly said, "Oh, don't pray for patience! God will send you trials"? The inference here is that being impatient is better than having to go through whatever it takes to make us patient. Impatience does not make the trials go away, however. They are inevitable. With this philosophy we remain impatient, but still have the trials. What about the added difficulties that result from impatience? Impatience is a killer. Clearly it is not a virtue.

Webster defines impatience as "a) feeling or showing annoyance because of delay, opposition, b) feeling or showing restless eagerness to do something, go somewhere...not willing to bear or tolerate." On the other hand, patience is the ability to wait without becoming annoyed, anxious, angry, or temperamental — to maintain possession of our souls.

When things do not go our way, we tend to get impatient: to manipulate, contrive, lie, rush, push, bang on the horn — whatever it takes to make it happen.

Here are some comparisons that will hopefully encourage you not only to pray for patience, but also to practice it.

Impatience is a deed of the flesh. Patience is a fruit of the Holy Spirit. "But the fruit of the Spirit is love, joy, peace, longsuffering [patience], kindness, goodness, faithfulness [faith], gentleness, self-control. Against such there is no law." Galatians 5:22-23.

Impatience is rushing ahead of time, being pushy, and being in a hurry. Patience is being content and restful.

Impatience is fear, doubt, and unbelief. Patience is faith in God.

Impatience tries to take matters into its own hands. Patience trusts God's timing in all things.

Impatience is a restless, boisterous spirit. Patience is a quiet and gentle spirit.

Impatience is reckless. Patience is cautious.

Impatience is lawless. Patience is lawful.

Impatience is rebellion. Patience is obedience and submissiveness.

Impatience is a proud spirit. Patience is a humble spirit. "Better is the end of a thing than the beginning thereof: and the patient in spirit is better than the proud in spirit." Ecclesiastes 7:8.

Impatience bears the fruit of anger, frustration, and fighting. Patience is a peacemaker.

Impatience curses. Patience blesses.

Impatience is self-centered. Patience is other-centered.

Impatience is trusting in one's own understanding. Patience leans not upon one's own understanding, but seeks the knowledge and understanding which is from God.

Impatience is talkative and interruptive, and has no ears to hear. Patience is a good listener.

Impatience is costly. Patience has its rewards.

Impatience is dangerous and destructive. Patience is the practice of safety.

Impatience and impetuousness are the nature of the old fallen man nature of flesh and sin. Patience is the righteous nature of God.

Impatience is losing hope in the Lord. Patience is maintaining hope in the Lord despite despair. "Now faith is the substance of things hoped for, the evidence of things not seen." Hebrews 11:1.

Patience takes time, so take time to wait upon the Lord.

Possess your soul in patience. Luke 21:19. "Let us run with endurance [patience] the race that is set before us." Hebrews 12:1. "Knowing this that the testing of your faith produces patience. But let patience have its perfect work, that you may be perfect and complete, lacking nothing." James 1:3-4.

12

LIBERTY IN FORGIVENESS

If I accidentally bumped into you and startled you with no harm done, then it is enough to simply say, "I'm sorry." Or, "Excuse me, please." There are times, however, when saying "I'm sorry" doesn't get it. Simply saying, "I'm sorry," leaves us open for the offended person to simply agree, "Yea! You are sorry!" Still, we can brush it off and move on.

To say, "I apologize" requires a little more humility than saying, "Sorry." Such apologies carry more weight than being sorry, and are often necessary for those times we ruffle someone else's feathers. An apology expresses regret for a wrong that we did against another.

As difficult as it is to say "sorry" or "I apologize," it almost stretches us beyond possible to say, "Forgive me." Yet, no other word will do in the face of the certain wounds we inflict upon each other. It is equally difficult to forgive another who has caused us pain.

Because it is difficult to ask forgiveness from others or to forgive others, many of us find bitterness taking root in our own hearts—eating away at our emotional, spiritual, and often physical well-being. The lack of forgiveness we harbor against another often holds us hostage to the offence more than it does the offending person. It never produces life and liberty.

We can say, "I'm sorry" or "I apologize," but the other party is not obligated to respond. On the other hand, when we ask forgiveness, it not only humbles us, but it also puts the offended person in a position of having to respond. The offended one does not have to forgive, but he can no longer remain passive. Some response is called for. He either forgives or chooses not to forgive. Failure to act is in itself a choice.

Healing from an offense cannot begin until we deal with this forgiveness factor. Forgiveness has to come from a sincere heart. It is always partnered with humility and a change of attitude. We cannot use it to manipulate others to get our way.

True forgiveness streams from a heart that desires never to inflict this offense again. True forgiveness is defined by a sincere change of mind that leads to a change of behavior.

Forgiveness is a Kingdom principle. Where do we ever hear Jesus saying, "Go tell that person you are sorry" or "You need to apologize to that person." Neither does it say that our heavenly Father accepts our apologies. "Oops! I am so sorry, God." He forgives those who ask for forgiveness.

Jesus taught in Matthew 6:14-15. "For if you forgive men their trespasses, your heavenly Father will also forgive you. But if you do not forgive men their trespasses, neither will your Father forgive your trespasses."

Does this mean God can hold unforgiveness toward us? Not at all! God is by His very nature a forgiving God. He holds forgiveness in His outstretched hand, deeply desiring for us to accept it, but He cannot release it to an unforgiving person. Consequentially, we withhold it from ourselves.

We need to come to that place in Jesus where there is neither the desire in our hearts to violate another nor hold unforgiveness toward another person. If we do harbor unforgiveness, let us humble ourselves and be quick to forgive. Let us be just as quick to forgive, even if the offending person has not asked for it. Forgiveness or the failure to ask forgiveness is a powerful force. Unforgiveness is bondage; forgiveness sets is free.

And that, my friend, is liberty in forgiveness.

13

MATURITY

The Big Book of Alcoholics Anonymous hits the bulls eye stating, "Selfishness, self-centeredness! That, we think, is the root of our troubles." Imagine that! We do not have to be an addict to know that is true. We are born sweet little innocent, precious, none-the-less self-absorbed infants.

Self-centeredness is often reinforced during our formative years. Consider the stressed out mom shopping with the little spitfire, screaming to the top of his lungs for that dazzling impulse item on the shelf. Out of desperation or the inability to say "no," she buys it to shut him up. Ah! Now he knows how to get his way! We expect this correctable behavior from children, but at some point, the earlier the better, they are supposed to grow up.

Self-centered persons are not fun to be around. They are toxic and drag you down—black holes in their little universe, sucking everything around them into themselves. Contrast this with self-giving persons who are nourishing and uplifting to be around. Would you not rather be one of them?

Self-centeredness is immaturity. As we mature, we are expected to become more other-centered. We become aware that it really is not all about "me." We become more giving, more caring, more loving, more nourishing to be around. We learn that our purpose in life is not to "get," but to "give."

Jesus taught, "Give and it shall be given unto you." Luke 6:38. Though "getting" should not be our motive for giving, it often seems to come back around to us.

Here is one sure way we can tell when young people are growing up: they see things to be done and do them without having to be asked. They help clear the table after dinner. They volunteer to take out the trash. They ask, "How was your day?" And take the time to listen.

Jesus made an astounding statement. He said, "Therefore you shall be perfect, just as your Father in heaven is perfect." Matthew 5:48. Even as God is perfect!? Now how in the world can anyone achieve that? Perhaps the meaning of the word in Greek can help us. It means: "to be full grown, adult, of full age, mature." It simply means, "Grow up!" We are to grow up into Christ in all things. Ephesians 4:15.

Children are self-centered. To become a mature son or daughter in the Kingdom of God is to become Father-centered. Jesus is the highest definition of a mature son. In the giving of His own life, He pleased the Father. He was Father-centered crying out, "Not My will, but Yours be done." Luke 22: 42.

Can you imagine Jesus throwing a conniption fit to get His way? Had He any thread of self-centeredness in Him, He could not have suffered the cruelty of the cross for our sins (not His, ours).

Without doubt, we need to grow up out of our childish

self-centeredness and become other-centered adults, especially focused on what God wants.

Desire to turn your focus away from yourself and consider the needs of others. Desire for others what is in their best interest. What a different atmosphere this would create in your sphere of influence!

Do not read this and think about all the other people who need to read this article. Rather, inventory yourself and ask, "In what ways am I self-centered and need to grow up?" "How can I consider others above myself today?" Then live it! You might just find yourself living a more joyful, peaceful, people-friendly lifestyle.

14

TRY JESUS

Try Jesus. If you don't like him, the devil will take you back.

I read the above on a church sign. Catchy for sure! And it is true, the devil will always take you back, but let us talk about the "try Jesus" part.

Is Jesus a commodity that we can simply try out like we might try out a new favorite flavor of ice cream? Or trying on a garment to find out if it fits us or not? If we do not like Him or if He does not work for us, can we simply return Him to "customer service"?

Can you imagine Jesus saying to the crowd on a mountainside, "Hey, guys, take me for a test drive and see how you like Me. Check out the new features in My Kingdom-of-God model."

I once heard someone say, "I tried that Jesus thing and it didn't work for me."

Read anywhere in the gospels and insert this concept into Jesus' narratives. Look at the passage in Luke 9:57-62 regarding three potential followers. What if the first man said,

"Lord, I will follow you wherever you go and if your deal works for me, I will keep on following." Do you think Jesus would have replied, "Sure, man, check out the other deals in town and get back with me if you want?" No, instead He made sure the man understood the consequences of following Him and said, "Foxes have holes and birds of the air have nests; but the Son of man has no where to lay His head." In other words, "Are you sure you want to pay the price to follow Me?"

Then Jesus called out to another man saying, "Follow Me." But the man said, "Let me first go and bury my father." Can you imagine Jesus saying, "Okay, man, I will wait for you here under this fig tree until after the funeral. I want to make this as easy as possible for My followers." Rather, Jesus said, "Let the dead bury their dead: but you go and preach the kingdom of God." Do we expect Jesus to follow us and bless the works of our hands? That is hardly the same as following Jesus.

Another man declared his willingness to follow Jesus, but wanted to go tell his family goodbye. Again, imagine Jesus saying, "Whatever, man. Whenever it suits you jump on the wagon." Rather, Jesus answered, "No man, having put his hand to the plow, and looking back, is fit for the kingdom of God."

The simple point to be made here is that Jesus is not Santa Claus or our errand boy. He has promised never to leave us, but His real intent is that we stick with Him, regardless. We are not to set forth a purpose for Him; He has a purpose for us. He does not follow us around; we follow Him. He is not a commodity to purchase for our pleasure; He purchased us for His pleasure.

Remember the guy who said he tried that Jesus thing and

IT didn't work? Please! Jesus is not an IT. He is not a religion. He is not a philosophy. He is not a doctrinal formula. He is the Person of the Godhead who desires a personal relationship with us. If we think of Him as something or someone to be tested and proven before accepted we will always be disappointed.

"Try Jesus!" I don't think so! Let us put our hands to the plow and not look back.

15

DASHED HOPES

Had any dashed hopes lately?

I had a few. When that happens we get frustrated, angry, depressed, or even vindictive.

Jackson sat across the table from me at lunch with tears in his eyes. "I was shocked at the outcome of the election," he said. Remorsefully, he added. "I was sure it would turn out differently." He had placed his hope in man, politics, political parties, government, and ideologies resulting in dashed hope.

In times of severe loss we may lash out at something or someone—even God. "Why did you let this happen? This is not how we prayed. This is not what we had hoped for."

While it is probably not wise to lash out at God, He does not suffer from an inferiority complex. So, I doubt that He gets upset when we get angry with Him in the throes of sorrowful emotions. Though we do not always understand what He is doing, He always understands our frustrations.

Things happen that often loom as large as doomsday scenarios. When these expectations run afoul, we have to admit that we had misplaced hope. Why, then, all the emotions? We feel these losses so deeply because we had put our hope in something that did not have the ability to produce in the long run. *Misplaced hope is a precursor for dashed hope.*

Take a look at all the things in which we place our hope and ask, "Are these really things in which I can invest my hope? Are these the things in which I even want to put my hope?" It is one thing to make use of these things and quite another to become dependent upon them—to magnify them into gods.

There I was, face to face with several losses in my own life, asking the Lord for understanding. I soon found myself humming an old hymn I had sung in church hundreds of times growing up, the singing of which had been little more than a religious exercise. This time, however, it came alive to me.

I dusted off an old hymnal on our library shelf and looked up the words. The Lord used these words to remind me that my hope is not in anyone, anything, or any institution, rather in Him and in Him alone. Maybe for the first time these words by Edward Mote (1797-1874) truly came alive to me.

"My hope is built on nothing less than Jesus' blood and righteousness. I dare not trust the sweetest frame, but wholly lean on Jesus name." Then came the chorus. I felt the urge to sing it to the top of my voice in order to be heard above the crescendo of a glorious orchestra that resounded in my spirit. "On Christ the solid rock I stand. All other ground is sinking sand. All other ground is sinking sand." I'm holding back tears of joy even as I write.

I do not build my hope upon the politicians, governments, or government handouts even though I receive certain services. I do not build my hope upon hospitals, doctors, and medicine, even though I gratefully use them as needed. I do not build my hope upon the stock market, though we have investments. I do not build my hope upon my job, my reputation, or my performance.

When "my hope is built on nothing less than Jesus' blood and righteousness," it can never be dashed again.

"Now may the God of hope fill you with all joy and peace in believing, that you may abound in hope, through the power of the Holy Spirit." Romans 15:13.

16

REFORMING OLD SYSTEMS

God is not remotely interested in reforming the old systems of men's inventions whether religious, political, financial, educational, social, or such. He is interested in replacing those systems of men with His Kingdom of righteousness, peace, and joy.

Jesus showed absolutely no interest in changing the political system of His day by political means. He preached that the Kingdom He came to establish was within the hearts and lives of men and women everywhere.

Is not that really the only way we will see a difference in our societies—when the rule of God is resident in the hearts and lives of people? Without His rule securely established in our hearts we can only argue our points of view and try to change each other's minds. It rarely works.

If we truly want to see change for a better life in the world around us, we will want to reach the heart and soul of individuals in the world with the gospel of the Kingdom of God. Any attempt to win the minds of men through argumentation will prove futile in the end.

What, then, is the gospel we preach? It was simply stated by Jesus who said, "If any man will come after Me, let him deny himself, and take up His cross, and follow Me." Matthew 16:24.

Where did Jesus go that we should follow Him? He went to the cross in the complete denial of Self. He was the perfect Lamb of God who was slain for us that we, the little imperfect lambs of God, through faith in Him, might be saved. We are being conformed into His image by the work of His Holy Spirit within us.

The word gospel means, "good news." So, how is preaching the denial of self to follow Jesus good news? Simply this! Who wants to continue to live in this fallen state of sin, sickness, and darkness, knowing that the final payoff of sin is death? By faith in Jesus and going through to the resurrection side of the cross, we can live in righteousness, light, and eternal Life. But it takes going through the cross. Do not just keep coming to the foot of the cross for the forgiveness of sins in your life. Go through it! Get past those sins. Let Him change your life. As He changes lives one life at a time, we will see the changes we desire in the world around us. Transformed lives transform societies.

Reforming old unreliable institutions upon which we depend and to which be bow down as though they were gods is fruitless. Shall we strive, nevertheless, for a better world in which to live? Of course! Do we want to see His Kingdom come on earth as it is in heaven? You bet! That difference has to be lived out from within us.

Remember the little boy whose parent told him to sit down? After a bit of protesting, he sat down and then muttered, "I may be sitting down on the outside, but I am still standing up on the inside." The rule of God on the inside of us is that which can revolutionize the world.

While civil laws are needed for lawless people, the Kingdom of God cannot be legislated outwardly. It has to be written in our hearts and lived out in our lives. We seek transformation, not mere reformation—lives being transformed by the blood of the Lamb one soul at a time. Therefore, "Shine as lights in the world." Philippians 2:15.

17

GENIE IN A BOTTLE

What if God were a genie in a bottle and He told you that you could have three wishes? What would they be? Caution! Your answer will reveal your heart.

"Three wishes, eh! I better think it through. Fame? Fortune? Power? Position? Recognition? Health?" Though our wishes might vary, one thing is predictable. We are more likely to wish for something for Self. Perhaps, in a more altruistic moment, we might spend one wish on someone else.

Yet, we dare ask, "What would God want for us to want?" I think God wants us to want what He wants from us. (Maybe you should read that again. Slower.)

The Bible reveals much about what God desires from us. The Old Testament is replete with urgings for us to "Seek the Lord." "Praise Him." "Worship the Lord with all your might." "Enter into His gates with singing and into His courts with praise."

"Okay," you might answer, "I go to church every Sunday morning and sing hymns of praise to Him. On occasions, I even put on worship CDs in my house or car." Nah! That is not what the Lord is looking for. He desires that continuous praise that comes from deep within the heart.

Jesus told the Samaritan woman at the well, "But the hour is coming, and now is, when the true worshipers will worship the Father in spirit and truth; for the Father is seeking such to worship Him." John 4:23. But we ask, "How can I worship God in spirit and truth when there is nothing in me capable of doing that? What does that even mean?" Truth is, we cannot do that on our own. We desperately need the enablement of His precious Holy Spirit within us to be the source of such praise. Ask Him to enable you.

Then, empowered by His Holy Spirit from on high, we may often find ourselves praising and worshipping God in a manner we never thought possible, not just on Sundays, but at extraordinary times throughout the week.

God deserves our highest praise and is altogether worthy of our worship. Certainly, He knows that we need to praise and worship Him more than He needs to be worshipped. Nevertheless, that is not the issue!

His Word as contained in the Bible makes it clear that we are to give priority to our praise and worship of Him. Thus we ask, "Is praise and worship of Him by any chance my priority? Is my praise and worship of Him more important than fame, fortune, power, position, recognition or any other thing that I might seek for myself?"

Given the choice to either win the multi-million dollar lottery or to have the enabling presence of God's Holy Spirit that we might worship Him in spirit and in truth—and we could not have both—for what would we ask? I know. I hesitated also. You see how earthly minded we are?

Yet, in the grand sweep of things, when our hearts are in

sync with God's, we would spend our first wish on the ability to praise Him in spirit and truth.

We should be thankful God is not a genie in a bottle and we do not make wishes to Him. He is not present to meet our every demand. He desires to be present within us that we might have that blessed fellowship with Him as a loving Father would have with loving sons and daughters.

Let us "Give unto the LORD the glory due to His name; worship the LORD in the beauty of holiness." Psalm 29:2.

18

REVIVAL OR REVOLUTION

Many people are praying for revival. Given the realities of the spiritual, moral, and social decay engulfing us, we know something needs to change.

However, I question the need for revival. The term revival is used in reference to an evangelistic meeting intended to reawaken interest in religion. The idea of revival suggests that we return to something we once had. Yet we ask, is what we once had really what we want to go back to?

If what we once had now needs reviving, then why would we expect it to not need reviving again in the future? To have to revive something suggests that it has weakened or even died. If that which we had can die, then I question that it was the real thing to begin with. The life we have in Christ Jesus is eternal. It does not die.

We generally want revival for the wrong reasons. We want to return to a time past that serves our memory with pleasantries. We may want to pump new life into our church. Perhaps we hope to change the political landscape to suit our liking. Whatever the reasons, they are usually self-serving. Revival has much to do with what we want.

Perhaps then, we need a spiritual revolution rather than revival. Revolution brings about a drastic and far-reaching change in how we think and behave. Our behavior changes as our thinking changes. This kind of change is what the Bible calls repentance. True repentance is the genesis of a true and lasting spiritual revolution.

Historically, repentance has thought to mean to turn away from our sins — to stop doing bad things and start living right. As if we could do that in our own strength! The true meaning of repentance, however, as used in the Bible is different from this. It has to do with changing our minds in such a radical way that it changes our behavior, our direction.

The spiritual revolution we need to be praying for has to do entirely with what God intends to have. God has not changed in what he intends. We need to find out what he intends and change our minds to be in agreement with him. That will be so radically different from the way we now think and do things that it will spark a spiritual revolution.

Think about it. Jesus came preaching that the kingdom of heaven is at hand. That was revolutionary then just as it is today. Jesus was not interested in revival.

His message was not about restoring the religion of His day to that "old-time religion." He was not interested in establishing a political kingdom of Israel to overthrow the Romans. He was not about pronouncing His blessing on the idolatrous kingdoms of men. His message was anchored in this phrase "you have heard it said of old...but I say to you...." Everything he said pointed to a new and different mindset.

We do not need to revive the old religious ways of performance in order to appease God. We need such a revolution that takes us all the way back to that simple step of obedience when, as the Master passes by and calls our name to come follow Him, we drop everything and go. It has never been about us. It is all about Jesus—who He is, what He wants, and what He intends to have in establishing His Kingdom on earth as it is in heaven.

Rather than praying for revival, pray for a spiritual revolution—one that begins with us.

19

JESUS PLUS NOTHING

A preacher once boasted, "I preach faith, and *it* works." I did not respond. Perhaps I should have said, "I preach Christ crucified, and *He* works."

In 1 Corinthians 1:22-24, Paul, the apostle, was the first to claim, "I preach Christ crucified." He was arguing against the teachings of certain Jewish converts to Christ who had wormed their way into the belief system of new Gentile believers. They were preaching Christ plus circumcision— proclaiming that the non-Jewish believers had to first be circumcised as Jews in order to be of Christ. These false teachers were referred to as Judaizers, or The Circumcision Party. They were teaching Christ plus something else.

Paul wrote, "O foolish Galatians! Who has bewitched you that you should not obey the truth, before whose eyes Jesus Christ was clearly portrayed among you as crucified?" Galatians 3:1.

This is the trend if we do not carefully guard the truth of the gospel (good news) of Jesus Christ: When we preach "Christ plus something", it soon reverses into "something plus Christ." Left unchecked, it becomes "something plus nothing." Then the other something becomes another gospel. Christ is omitted altogether. That is not good news! Ultimately, though, when we come to understand the fullness and sufficiency of Christ in us, we will resolve to preach, "Christ plus nothing."

The "something else" we tend to add to the good news of Jesus Christ may be the outgrowth of a true revelation or teaching that the Holy Spirit has given. It usually has an element of truth in it. Yet, when we legalize it, preach it as essential to our salvation, and make it the gospel we preach, we are preaching another gospel; thereby, making the word of God of no effect through our traditions. Mark 7:13.

These teachings stretch across the spectrum of our religious traditions, rituals, doctrines, codes of dress and behavior, and supposed revelations; such things as: Christ plus our brand of denominationalism, Christ plus church government, Christ plus church membership, Christ plus the sacraments, Christ plus the Rapture, Christ plus prosperity, Christ plus observing Hebraic feasts and Sabbaths, or Christ plus works of any kind. The list is extensive! The deception is subtle!

These are the issues that divide us, enslave us, and lure us away from our first love—Jesus. Think about the last religious argument you heard. The issues being argued were most likely over one of those "plus something" kinds of things. Both sparring partners were in error if they were contending for something other than the simplicity and purity of devotion to Jesus. Have you ever fallen out with another believer over your love for Jesus?

Certainly, we may receive divine and up-building revelations that need to be preached, believed, and practiced.

Nevertheless, we ask: Does it point to Jesus or to itself? Does it liberate or hold believers hostage to laws of our own making?

Many demonically inspired false teachings are blindsiding seasoned teachers and well-meaning believers today. We want to be discerning, remembering that in the last days "there will be false teachers among you, who will secretly bring in destructive heresies..." 2 Peter 2:1.

We are in safe harbor when we stick to preaching Jesus Christ crucified. Jesus plus nothing!

"Stand fast therefore in the liberty by which Christ has made us free, and do not be entangled again with a yoke of bondage." Galatians 5:1.

20

WHO DOES YOUR LIFE SAY THAT I AM?

How often have we heard the cliché, "Action speaks louder than words." St. Francis of Assisi is credited with saying, "Preach the Gospel at all times. Use words if necessary."

Jesus hiked His twelve apostles to Caesarea Philippi one day and asked them, "Who do men say that I, the Son of man, am?" "Some say John the Baptist." "Some say Elijah." Then another answered, "Some say, Jeremiah or one of the prophets." He then asked them, "But who do you say that I am?" Peter declared, "You are the Christ, the Son of the living God." Jesus assured Peter that he did not figure this out on his own, but that God had revealed it to him. Matthew 16:13-20.

I was listening to Don Potter's song based on this passage of scripture in which he cries out, "Who do you say that I am?" It came to me to ask it this way, "Who does your life say that I am?" This is different from what Jesus asked, but I think it is a legitimate question. Do you?

But what does this mean? How can our lives preach the

gospel without using words? "I try to live a godly life." "I try to live by the Ten Commandments." "I go to church, give to missions, do charitable work when I can." "I try to set a good example." "I doubled my tip and left a salvation tract for the server at the cafe." These appear to be pious things to do, but they do not satisfactorily answer the question. Any good person can do these things, whether Christian or otherwise.

Jesus instructed His followers in John 13:35 saying, "By this all will know that you are My disciples, if you have love for one another." This would go a long way toward a satisfactory answer to our question if only we knew the kind of love spoken of here. It was the kind of love that Jesus defined in John 15:13. "Greater love has no man than this, than to lay down one's life for his friends." This is the kind of love He demonstrated by His own life and death on the cross.

If this is the answer, we are really in trouble. We do not seem to know how to love that way.

This question has to be answered on an individual basis. "Who does *my* life say that Jesus Christ is?" May I suggest that the answer can only come by living our lives according to this motto: "All things by the Spirit." That is, do all things according to the leading of the Holy Spirit in your life, presuming He is in your life.

As we ask to be filled with the Holy Spirit and learn to be led by the Spirit in all things, we will reveal the heart and will of the Father. We will be what God has made us to be. We will say what God wants us to say. We will do what God wants us to do. And yes, we will love one another as He commanded.

Then, through these acts of loving obedience, people will

be able to witness the kind of God we have living in us—the kind of God living His kind of life out from within us. People can slough off our religious words and actions, but they will see who Jesus is through our Spirit-led actions—even those that require words.

21

THE FINISHED WORK OF GOD

Jesus declared in John 5:17-36 that He and the Father (God) had been working up until then. He further claimed that He only did what He saw the Father doing. Then, He added that He was the work of God. He was what Father was doing. Moreover, He declared that He was the finished work of God.

His listeners asked what they needed to do to work the works of God. They were only familiar with the burdensome works that their religious leaders had required of them. It would have been natural for them to expect Jesus to give them another "to do" list. Surprisingly, He did not! Instead He answered, "This is the work of God that you believe in Him whom He sent." John 6:28-29. What? That's it? Yes, that's it! God's job is to do all that is necessary for us to be saved and our job is to truly believe in Him.

The last words Jesus spoke on the cross were, "It is finished." He was declaring that He had finished the work the Father had sent Him to accomplish. Once we truly get a grip on all the works that Jesus finished for our benefit, as witnessed in scripture, then our confession will be something like the following:

He is our Savior and our salvation; therefore, by faith in His finished work on the cross, we *are* saved.

He is our redeemer and our redemption; therefore, by faith in His finished work on the cross, we *are* redeemed.

He is our justifier and our justification; therefore, by faith in His finished work on the cross, we *are* justified.

He is our deliverer and our deliverance from evil; therefore, by faith in His finished work on the cross, we *are* delivered.

He is our health and our healing; therefore, by faith in His finished work on the cross, we *are* healed.

He is our sanctifier and our sanctification (the separated life); therefore, by faith in His finished works on the cross, we *are* sanctified.

He is our glory and our glorification; therefore by faith in His finished work on the cross, we *are* glorified.

Jesus is the author and finisher of our faith, the shepherd and guardian of our soul, the apostle and high priest of our confession. He is our Lord, our God, our king, our master in charge of everything.

These are not just litanies from the back of our hymnals, but the convictions of our hearts.

Everything that Jesus did comes out of who He is. He comes as an all-inclusive package. We cannot cherry pick what aspects of His works suit us. When we receive Him, we receive all of who He is and what He accomplished. For now we see in part; yet, we choose to believe in full.

We receive the glorious blessings of His finished works

by grace through faith. Ephesians 2:8. Grace is the power of God that enables us to be what He has made us to be and to do what He has called us to do. The declaration of our faith releases the power of God's grace. This grace is not a license to sin. It is our deliverance from sin — our power to choose, our desire to live holy and righteous lives.

Therefore, the Lord is worthy of our highest praise and worship, all honor, glory, riches and power belong to Him. He is our sovereign Lord, God, and King.

What a mighty God we serve!

22

WHOSE ARE YOU?

The church marquee read, "Know whose you are more than who you are." I gave it a 'thumbs up' as I drove on past.

As far back as the 1960's, many people sat around contemplating their navels asking, "Who am I?" Some still do that. Many answers were babbled about, but none settled well — like the bewildered trying to lead the bewildered.

Years ago a young man aggressively whisked past my car and cut in front of me on his way to wherever. I felt the impact of his rage and asked the Lord, "Why are so many people angry today?" The answer came surprisingly quick. "Because they do not know who they are."

At the time, I was writing the book *In Search of Dad* and had come to believe that we are who our fathers say we are. Sadly, many fathers dropped out over the past generations and failed to confirm their children, especially the sons who were to pass the blessing to future generations.

(I exhort you fathers to step up to the plate. Affirm, confirm, and validate your children. Bless them and never curse them. You have the God-given authority to say who they are. Who you say they are is who they most likely will believe themselves to be. This works both in a positive and negative way. So, be careful what you say and how you say it.)

God, the Father, through His Holy Spirit, affirmed Jesus, His only begotten Son, saying, "This is My beloved Son in whom I am well pleased." Matthew 3:17. This was the portal through which Jesus entered His glorious ministry as the Son of God and shaped His destiny as well as ours. He knew who He was because He knew whose He was. Nothing could shake that reality.

Every true believer in Christ Jesus, likewise, needs the assurance from Father-God that "You are My beloved son (male and female), in whom I am well pleased." We can only come to know this as His Spirit bears witness with our spirits that we are the children of God. Romans 8:16.

Jesus made clear, while praying to the Father, "That they [we] all may be one; as You, Father, are in Me, and I in You, that they [we] also may be one in us." John 17:21.

He is the Son of God and by grace through faith we have become the sons of God. We are not our own. We have been bought with a price. 1 Corinthians 6:20; 7:23. We belong to Him. We know who we are because we know whose we are.

Being a Christian is more than maintaining a detached religious expression toward God. It is not just about getting saved so we will miss hell and go to heaven. Our Heavenly Father has a much grander view of us than this.

Ask the Father to reveal to you exactly whose you are. He wants us to know that. We are His sons and we are to bear His image, likeness and character. This knowledge humbles us and is not something over which we become prideful.

Once we come to know whose we are, we will be unshakable in knowing who we are. We who come to know this will no longer sit around musing, "Who am I?"

Rather, we will rejoice with wonderment beholding, "What manner of love the Father has bestowed upon us, that we should be called the children [sons] of God." 1 John 3:1.

23

FINISHING WELL

Every person's life is a story. While we may yet have a few more chapters to write, I realize at seventy-seven years of age (in 2013) that my wife and I as a married couple are nearing the end of our story. We began the story of our marriage forty-three years ago. We would rewrite some of it if we could; nevertheless, what is written is written.

Though we never actually had a "bucket list," there are things we had hoped to do that we now know will not happen. We are surrendered to that. Nevertheless, we can still do some meaningful things—if nothing more than to enjoy what time we can 'loot' from life for ourselves.

We talked about how best to make the most of the remaining time. We thought about the things we needed to finish up, clean up, fix up, and give up.

This is not depressing to us because, as believers in Jesus Christ, another parallel story has been in the writing for the last thirty-five years. It began when we were converted to a life of following Jesus, but unlike our earthly story, it has no end. Death brings conclusion to this earthly story, but it is also the portal into eternal life. We are losing interest in clinging to this earthly, physical existence. Rather, we look forward to that time when we are in the presence of the Lord.

Nevertheless, before we end our earthly story, we want to make sure it finishes well. If we can do anything at all to end our story gloriously, we want to do that. My prayer: "Lord, make sure I end well. Make sure I end gloriously for the sake of your glory." Many people do not.

Then, I realized that we are not the only ones writing the climax to our story. Everyone in our extended families and relationships contribute to it. Each one will either jot down words that will bring comfort and cheer or unwanted drama. So, we may ask our children and those in our knit-work of relationships, and anyone else involved in our story, "How do you want to influence the remaining pages of our lives?"

Likewise, we realize that we still have time to add memories to the lives of those whose story will go on after ours is finished. How can we make a positive difference to them?

What about you? What influence will you bring to bear upon those you know who are in the final pages of their lives? You can pen goodness into their stories as well.

If you, too, are now writing the last pages of your life, make your bucket list if you can and enjoy checking it off while you can, but also look back upon those whose stories have as yet many pages to go. Plan to make the last words of your story as lovely as you can for yourself, but also for those you leave behind. Make amends and speak your blessings while a few blank pages remain. This could be your greatest legacy to them.

We contribute to each other's stories whether we think about it or not. So, give it serious thought and act accordingly, deliberately.

Paul, the apostle, wrote regarding the end of his story, "I have fought the good fight. I have finished the race. I have kept the faith." 2 Timothy 4:7.

The epitaph on my tombstone, should there be one, will be the final line in my storybook. May it simply read, "He finished well."

24

DARE TO BE LIGHT

I lit a candle and watched the tiny flame randomly flicker about. Neither did it cast a shadow nor shed much light. It was merely absorbed by the light of day.

As the light of day faded into the darkness of night, that little flicker of fire increasingly lit the room. The flame appeared to burn brighter, yet it was the same intensity as before.

The candlelight prevailed over the darkness. The darkness could not snuff out its light. It was interesting to see how a small flame of light could make such a difference. The greater the darkness, the greater the light!

Spiritually speaking of things in the world, the dark is getting darker and the light is getting lighter, and the dingy gray in between is disappearing. It will continue in this direction until we come to the end of this age. The Bible uses these terms often. All that pertains to the Kingdom of God is light. All else is considered darkness.

Jesus said, regarding believers in Him, that we are "the light of the world." Imagine that! He then added, "Nor do they light a lamp and put it under a basket, but on a lampstand, and it gives light to all who are in the house." Matthew 5:13,14.

Jesus intends for us to be light in a dark world. He is the light of the world. We are lights in the world. His light within us shines through us.

Have you noticed how gradually the darkness crept upon us and how suddenly it seems to have engulfed us? We no longer call sin, sin. Almost everything in our society is being redefined to suit our notions of political correctness and social acceptance. Evil appears to triumph over good. We feel powerless.

Men grope in darkness. They lose their way, their sense of direction, their grip on reason, their measuring stick for morality, and their hunger for righteousness. They do what they think is right in their own sight. They wag their fingers at God. They bow their knees to the gods of their own making. Yes. These are such times. The dark is getting darker.

We desperately desire to cling to what we have thought to be the day. But do you not see? The darkness must come in order to shake us from our complacency and reveal the light of Christ. As this darkness thickens, those who are lights in the world will not only shine brighter, but will also light the paths of many who repent from the darkness.

Here is the catch, though. To be a candle set on a hill, we have to be willing to be set on fire and to be diminished, though never extinguished. We have to be willing to face the taunts and evil workings of the darkness that is in the world—willing even to face martyrdom. Jesus promised it. John 15:20. That is a daunting fact to face, but consider the options: to either be light amidst darkness or to be lost in that darkness.

No more lukewarm. No more fence straddling. We ask the Lord to set us on fire and go forward lest we drift back into the darkness.

Paul, the apostle wrote, "For you were once darkness, but now you are light in the Lord. Walk as children of light." Ephesians 5:8. Also read 1 Thessalonians 5:4-6.

Dare to be light and make a difference!

25

DUH!

D uh! Doesn't everybody already know that?

Probably, but it did not "hit" me until recently when I realized that in the natural, physical realm everything ages and sooner or later everything dies. Every-thing—trees, plants, animal life, buildings, automobiles, all our toys, the earth! It all perishes, sooner or later. Everything turns to moth and rust. Matthew 6:19-21.

"So?" Well, think about how liberating that is to know, especially as believers in Jesus Christ! Once that concept sinks in, we do not have to be driven to find the fountain of youth, invent that age-defying formula, or waste time and money on facelifts or tummy tucks. We do not have to fret when we discover the horror that our skin is no longer at-tached to our bodies. We do not have to fear the angel of death. We get to "mature" gracefully.

Even people Jesus healed and raised from the dead con-tinued to age and sooner or later died. Of course, He did not heal anyone for vanity's sake. Countless numbers of people over the centuries have received miraculous healings from the Lord. Yet, they continued to age and sooner or later died. "It is appointed for men to die once...." Hebrew 9:27.

Perhaps everyone already realizes this inevitability, yet we seem predisposed to try to defy it. We have such a perverted sense of gain and loss. *We seek to gain the very things that are meant for loss while ignoring the very things that are meant for gain.* Jesus asked it this way: "For what profit is it to a man if he gains the whole world, and is himself destroyed or lost?" Luke 9:25.

Paul declared, "Even though our outward man is perishing, yet the inward man is being renewed day by day." 2 Corinthians 4:16. The soul and spirit of man are eternal. They do not die.

Nevertheless, most of us invest the bulk of our time, money, and energy on those things that are temporal (earthly, natural, physical)—things that are meant for loss. We seem at a loss to know how to go the gym of the Holy Spirit and exercise those things that are meant for gain.

Paul, the apostle, discovered that those things he once counted as gain to him, he later counted as loss for Christ. "For the excellence of the knowledge of Christ Jesus my Lord, for whom I have suffered the loss of all things, and count them as rubbish, that I may gain Christ." Philippians 3:7-8. He was referring to his knowledge of and position in his religious party.

When Christ apprehended Paul, his whole outlook on life radically changed. He became the very thing he was out to destroy. He became a believer in and follower of Jesus, Christ. He could say with great certainty, "For to me, to live is Christ, and to die is gain." Philippians 1:21.

What should be our priorities and what really matters in

the long haul?

No doubt we need to eat responsibly, exercise when we can, and take good care of our bodies—the temples of the Holy Spirit. However, I am saying for the most part in our western culture, we are obsessed with that which is going to age and sooner or later die. Rather, we need to totally surrender our lives to Jesus Christ and major on that which will not perish.

That reality needs to "hit" us all as well. That which pertains to the eternal, spiritual realm of the Kingdom of God never ages and never dies.

26

FREE TRIP TO HEAVEN: INQUIRE WITHIN

I love the little quips on church marquees. Some of them get me going. Here's one: "Free trip to Heaven: inquire within." I did not inquire within, but I'm pretty sure I know what the saying means. Depending of course upon your religious persuasion, it variously goes: Come to the altar, say the sinner's prayer, profess your faith, receive water baptism, "get saved," and be assured that "you're on your way to heaven." No mention of the cost of true discipleship.

True discipleship involves far more than "getting saved," going to church, giving tithes and offerings, while we go about living our self-involved lives. True discipleship costs you your life. This has to do with going through the cross. (Preachers beware! You cannot build a work on the cross. It is not popular.)

We have been programmed to believe that we can have it God's way while continuing to do our own thing. We will either do things God's way or our way, but not both. To do things God's way is to surrender one's self to God. To do things our way is to resist God's way. God's way leads to life; our way leads to death. The choice is ours just as it was with Joshua entering the Promised Land. He declared, "Choose for yourselves this day whom you will serve...But as for me and my house, we will serve the LORD." Joshua 24:15.

There is no such thing as a self-serving Christian. Jesus called His disciples to lay down their lives if they wanted to follow Him. We are either following Jesus or we are following self-will.

A lot of people call themselves Christian who continue to live self-willed, self-serving lives. This is one reason why the term "Christian" has such a bad reputation in the world and partly why some believers no longer even want to be labeled "Christian." Christians who live self-serving lives tremendously weaken the meaning of the word Christian. Perhaps also, this is one reason so many nonbelievers fail to see the merit of being a Christian.

Jesus made it challenging for individuals to follow Him. He told His followers that if they did not drink the blood and eat the flesh of the Son of man they had no life in them. This was such a hard saying that most of them turned away. He, then, asked His closest followers if they also wanted to turn back. "Simon Peter answered him, 'Lord, to whom shall we go? You have the words of eternal life.'" John 6:53-69.

The call to follow Christ is not a call to namby-pamby Christianity. It is the total surrender of life. It is the substitution of one life for another. Christ died that we might live. We surrender our lives to Him that He might live His life in and through us. Galatians 2:20.

Thankfully, we are not the judge of who goes to heaven and who does not. The question here is simply this, "What does it mean to be a true disciple of Jesus Christ?" And the answer is derived from this verse: "If any man desires to come after Me, let him deny himself, and take up his cross, and follow Me [Jesus]." Matthew 16:24. No man can serve two masters. You cannot serve God while living a self-serving life.

So, you want a free trip to heaven? Your ticket is punched as long as you are willing to go through the cross to get there. Resurrection life awaits beyond the cross.

27

TAPESTRY

Corrie Ten Boom wrote in her poem, *The Tapestry*, that she only saw what God was weaving in her life from the underside of dangling threads while He saw it from the topside of His finished artistry.

Being in the family of God is much like a tapestry. We are a beautiful knit-work of art that only the master designer of the universe could weave — one that would leave awestruck the most hardened heart if permitted to see it.

We are normally allowed to only see the underside of this tapestry. The fault-finder says, "Look at that, would you? Nothing but strings of threads dangling in the air." "And over there, what an ugly color! How could that ever fit in?" "I sure am glad I am not as stringy as that one over there." "Ah, now there is a golden piece of thread. I think I will move next to it. What? You don't want me next to you?"

Looking only at the underside of this tapestry, we might conclude that it is the most messed up, disjointed, ragged thing we have ever seen in our life. God, how could you ever make anything out of this mess you call the Body of Christ?

This is often the attitude we express toward one another in the body of Christ. We cannot see much beauty in it.

It is no wonder then that we have to be exhorted to "love one another." "Be kind one to another." "Serve one another." "Bear one another's burdens." "Forgive one another."

All of our misconceptions would vanish, were we granted the privilege to see the topside of this glorious tapestry — the finished work of God in Christ; namely, His Bride.

"Remember that ugly color we saw underneath? Wow! Look how beautifully it accents the other threads woven into it on the upper side!"

Without a doubt, we will get to see the glory side of this tapestry in heaven. But why wait? The Lord instructed us to pray for the Kingdom of God to come on earth as it is in heaven. If we already have a hint of how things will be in heaven, why not practice it now while on earth? If you really believe that both you and your neighbor with whom there is animosity will end up in heaven, then for heaven's sake, stop the animosity now. Exercise the Kingdom on earth now.

Stop judging yourself, others, and the body of Christ by what you see on the earthly underside. Pray for God to allow you to know one another from the heavenly topside. Why would any of us want to live from the underside of life anyway?

It takes a measure of faith to look at life this way. We have to believe what God in His written word says about us and how we should live in relationship with one another. Allow the truth contained in the Bible to prove itself in your life.

If the Bible says to turn the other cheek, then turn the other cheek. It is a beautiful thing. If the Bible says to give, then give. It is a beautiful thing. If the Bible says to love your neighbor, then love your neighbor. It is a beautiful thing. The Bible says we are being knit together in love. Colossians 2:2. Believe it and make it happen. It is a beautiful thing.

From where God sits, that tapestry is already finished. We cannot unravel what God has woven.

28

IMPOSSIBLE RESOLUTIONS

Do people still make New Year's resolutions? Did you? I gave up on that many years ago. I simply did not have the willpower within myself to keep those promises. I had resolved to do the impossible.

Those resolutions were my plans for me, but I discovered God has a different plan. Paul, the apostle, phrased it this way. "For this is the will of God, your sanctification." 1 Thessalonians 4:3.

Ok! I've heard that big theological term tossed about all my Christian life. Sanctification—what does it mean? Does this involve a long list of dos and don'ts that will just make me feel bad about myself for not being able to abide by them?

The term has often been interpreted legalistically and applied to outward behavior and appearances. There are scriptures that could be read suggesting such, but are these interpretations in step with the whole counsel and spirit of the New Testament of grace through faith? May it be according to the conviction of your inner voice!

Nevertheless, we do not want to miss the deeper meaning of sanctification and holiness by assigning it exclusively to religious codes of outward behavior and appearances.

Certainly, sanctification is God's will. It means "separation" or "set apart." We, as true believers in Jesus, are to be a separated people—set apart from the world, the domain of Satan, and from the deeds of our sinful nature. Galatians 5:19-21.

We are not only to be separated *from* these evil things. We are to be separated *unto* God. God really wants that. The only way we can be separated *from* any of this evil in the world is to first be separated *unto* God. This separated life is His will for us. A sanctified life is glorious. It should never be a burden on our backs, but we cannot separate ourselves.

Being separated unto God is the Holy Spirit's job that begins when we are born again and continues on as we willfully allow Him to cleanse and purify us from all sin and the works of the flesh. It continues until we are brought to that place of completion, maturity, and perfection that is found in Christ Jesus—"Till we all come in the unity of the faith, and of the knowledge of the Son of God, unto a perfect man, unto the measure of the stature of the fullness of Christ." Ephesians. 4:13.

We are expected to act differently, look differently, and talk differently because we are different from the world. This sanctification does not work from the outside in. We are not sanctified by what we do. Rather, it is accomplished from the inside out. What we do is the result of God's work from within. It is God's work in us, and not our work in us. We are His workmanship and not our own. Ephesians. 2:10.

Nevertheless, His work within us gives the power to live

a sanctified life. We are to "know how to possess our vessels in sanctification and honor...." 1 Thessalonians 4:4.

As you reflect upon any good-intended resolutions you may have made, be sure to include this one:

"Lord, I resolve to the best of my ability to turn my life and my will over to your complete care and will. I resolve to live a separated, set-apart, holy life—one that is befitting a believer in Jesus Christ. I will do the possible. You do the impossible."

29

VELVETY SOFT CHEEK

Wylie was less than two weeks old when I first met him. He is my third great-grandchild. And I do mean "great." How absolutely precious! Are they not all? (Forgive the doting.) He lay quietly snuggled in my lap, swaddled in his baby blanket, totally oblivious to the hurdles he would have to clear in the years to come.

I gently stroked his velvety soft cheek with the tip of my forefinger and marveled, "How could anything be any sweeter and more innocent?" In contrast, I wondered how anyone could take such a life in order to harvest tissue to prolong his own life.

That triggered something in me. Extreme *selfishness* takes a life in an effort to save it's own. While, on the other hand, extreme *selflessness* would give up its life to save another.

The following day, as it happened, I checked my smart phone's Bible app for the verse of day. Coincidence? Perhaps! Then, perhaps not! The verses were Mark 8:34-35: "Whoever desires to come after Me, let him deny himself, and take up his cross, and follow Me. For whoever desires to save his life will lose it, but whoever loses his life for My sake and the gospel's will save it." *Selfishness* could never choose that way of life. *Selflessness* could.

After all, is that not what Jesus did? Is that not what He taught? "Greater love has no one than this, than to lay down one's life for his friends." John 15:13.

In this context, the Ten Commandments came to mind in a way I had not thought of before. The first four commandments have to do with our relationship with God. We are not to have any other gods before us, nor make and bow down to any carved image, nor take God's name in vain, and we are to keep the Sabbath day holy. Exodus 20:3-8.

The following six commandments have to do with our relationship with each other — we are to honor our parents; we are not to murder, commit adultery, steal, bear false witness, or covet. Exodus 20:12-17. These all have to do with selflessness.

Jesus summed up these two parts of the Ten Commandments by saying, "You shall love the LORD your God with all your heart, with all your soul, and with all your mind.' This is the first and great commandment. And the second is like it: 'You shall love your neighbor as yourself..'' Matthew 22:38-40.

The common factor in all Ten Commandments is love. This kind of love has to do with selfless living — the unconditional, sacrificial giving of oneself for what is in the best interest of another. We live selfless lives before God and among our fellow man. That is how we keep the Ten Commandments.

God demonstrated His selfless love toward us in that He gave His only begotten Son to die for us. Jesus, living in obedience to His Father's will, demonstrated His selfless love toward us in the sacrificial giving of His own life. Everything that conflicts with this kind of love is a violation of the nature and character of God.

God gives life. He does not take life for His own selfish reasons. Neither do we. It is not in our nature to want to do that, if indeed Christ is in us.

So thank you, Wylie. While still helplessly dependent upon another for your own nurture, God used you to teach a very important lesson in selfless living—through a gentle touch of the tip of my forefinger upon your velvety soft cheek.

30

FRUIT OF THE SPIRIT

"I wish they would hurry up with our food," Josh grumbled. It sounded like my kind of complaint. However, on this occasion, I decided to push him on it.

Patting him on the shoulder, I urged, "Patience, my man, patience. Patience is a virtue."

"Not after my day at work," he snapped back. "I don't have any patience."

I pushed on. "Patience is a fruit of the Spirit. If Jesus is in you as He says He is, then patience is in you. You just have to let Him be Him through you." I'm not sure he was in the mood to go along with that reasoning at the moment. Hunger can make you crazy. I changed the subject, but later began to think more seriously about our little chitchat.

The fruit of the Spirit includes more than patience. Paul, the apostle, wrote in Galatians 5:22-23, "The fruit of the Spirit is love, joy, peace, longsuffering (patience), kindness, goodness, faithfulness, gentleness, and self-control."

We know that a tree can only bear fruit according to its

own nature. James wrote, "Can a fig tree, my brethren, bear olives, or a grapevine bear figs?" James 3:12. When Jesus cautioned His followers to beware of false prophets, He said, "You will know them by their fruit. Even so, every good tree bears good fruit, but a bad tree bears bad fruit." Matthew 7:15-19. Jesus is the Tree of Life and He bears the fruit of the Spirit—love, joy, peace, et al. He determines the kind of fruit we bear because He is in us and we are in Him. John 14:20.

Before Christ came into us we were of the old man of flesh and sin nature. Paul contrasted the fruit of the Spirit with what he called the works (deeds) of the flesh—that old man of sin nature. They are such things as, "adultery, fornication, uncleanness, lewdness, idolatry, sorcery, hatred, contentions, jealousies, outbursts of wrath, selfish ambitions, dissensions, heresies, envy, murders, drunkenness, revelries." Galatians 5:19-21.

By this, then, we understand that the fruit of the Spirit does not and cannot come out of our old fallen man nature of flesh and sin. Even good works are not all life producing. Spirit-fruit cannot be forced to happen. Nothing in the tree of our old man nature can produce this kind of God-like fruit. We need to be of a different tree. That new nature tree is Jesus, the Tree of Life.

Therefore, we understand that the only way we can produce any of the fruit of the Sprit is for Jesus to live in us and work His life out from within us. That includes patience. He does this through the power life of His Holy Spirit in us. We call it the exchanged life.

Now then, the next time we think we are short on patience, or any of the fruit of the Spirit for that matter, we need to think again. If, indeed, Christ is in us and we are in Him as He says we are, then we have the potential to bear the fruit of the Spirit. Paul concluded, "And those who are Christ's have crucified the flesh with its passions and desires."

We cannot crucify the flesh in our own strength, but in the power of the Lord's resurrection life within us.

If we live in the Spirit, let us also walk in the Spirit." Galatians 5:24-25. If we walk in the Spirit, we will bear the fruit of the Spirit for the good of all.

31

THE LIFE OF THE TREE

The tree of life in Genesis 2 and the tree of life in Revelation 22 symbolically represent Jesus. He, as the Tree of Life, needs to be the life within our tree.

In Matthew 7:17-18, Jesus illustrated that "Every good tree bears good fruit, but a bad tree bears bad fruit." Furthermore, He said "A good tree cannot bear bad fruit, nor can a bad tree bear good fruit."

We see, then, that bad fruit does not make the tree bad. It is the other way around. A bad tree produces bad fruit. Likewise, good fruit does not make the tree good. The good tree produces good fruit. The fruit is the life of the tree. Jesus concluded, "You will know them by their fruit." Matthew 7:16. We can know a good tree from a bad tree by its fruit.

Therefore, it is not so much what we do, but who we are. We are either Sinners or righteous persons. Sinner speaks of who we are. We are not Sinners because we sin. We sin because we are Sinners. As Sinners, we are under the power of Sin (with a capital "S").

Righteousness, likewise, speaks of who we are. We are

not righteous because we do not sin or because we do righteous things. We do not sin because we are righteous. If we were made righteous because we do not sin, then our righteousness would be dependent upon our own works, thus snubbing our noses at the finished work of God in Christ.

People lie because they are Liars. The fact that one may have told a lie does not make that person a Liar. A righteous man may slip and lie, but because he is righteous and not a Liar, he will be burdened with conviction until the truth be told. Not so with a Liar! One sin does not make you a Sinner, just as one righteous deed does not make one righteous.

A Sinner lives according to the flesh. A righteous person lives according to the Spirit. We either live according to the flesh — the bad tree, or according to the Spirit — the good tree.

If we live according to the flesh, we will do the deeds of the flesh. These are such things as adultery, fornication, uncleanness, lewdness, idolatry, sorcery, hatred, contentions, jealousies, outbursts of wrath, selfish ambitions, dissensions, heresies, envy, murders, drunkenness, revelries... Galatians 5:19-21.

If we live according to the Spirit, we will bear the fruit of the Spirit. These are such things as love, joy, peace, long-suffering [patience], kindness, goodness, faithfulness, gentleness, and self-control. Galatians 5:22-23.

What is on the inside of us is what matters. Jesus exhorted the scribes and Pharisees, even calling them hypocrites. "For you cleanse the outside of the cup and dish, but inside they are full of extortion and self-indulgence...first cleanse the inside of the cup and dish, that the outside of them may be clean also." Matthew 23:25-26. Paul proclaimed that Christ in us is our hope of glory. Colossians 1:27.

"Either make the tree good and its fruit good, or else make the tree bad and its fruit bad; for a tree is known by its fruit." Matthew 12:33.

Ultimately, we need to know that "every tree that does not bear good fruit is cut down and thrown into the fire." Matthew 7:19.

The fruit is in the life of the tree. We need Jesus, the tree of life, flowing within the tree of our lives. Invite Him in.

32

IN WHOM WE BELIEVE

Christians are not saved by "in *what* we believe." We are saved by "in *whom* we believe." When we put it that way, it is hard to say, "It ain't so." Deep down we know it is.

Nevertheless, what we often hear preached and taught sounds like we are saved by "in *what* we believe." Pay attention to what is preached and taught. The whole body of Christ in the church world is divided over those "in *what* we believe" things. We call these things "doctrines (teachings)," "creeds," and "confessions of faith."

Christians share the common belief in the One in *whom* we all believe, Jesus Christ. He is the cornerstone of Christianity, the cornerstone of our faith.

Following that common belief, we divide over all of those "in *what* we believe" things. We become adamant about them and put our trust for salvation in them. So much so, that we might even dare to say, "Unless you believe as we do, you cannot be saved. You must believe as we believe and do as we do."

Putting our trust for our salvation in *what* we believe

rather than in *whom* we believe gets real sticky. We are hard pressed to find any two of us who agree on all that we think we know and believe.

Nevertheless, getting our doctrines right is necessary. Right doctrines produce life, light, and liberty. They include us all. False doctrines produce death, darkness, and bondage. They exclude others. Wrong and deceptive doctrines can wreak havoc upon our spiritual lives and potentially upon all aspects of our lives. The test of any true doctrine is that it points to the One who is the Truth—Jesus Christ.

We are not to camp out around our doctrines regardless of how right they may be. They should not be the basis for our fellowship. "Our fellowship is with the Father and with His Son Jesus Christ." 1 John 1:3. If what we believe divides us, it is most likely one of those doctrines that we believe can save us.

Our doctrines did not die on the cross. They did not shed precious undefiled blood for our redemption. They did not rise victoriously from the grave. They did not ascend into heaven where they sit at the right hand of the Father. They did not and cannot save us.

The Bible states it very simply. "For God so loved the world that He gave His only begotten Son, that whoever believes in Him should not perish but have everlasting life." John 3:16. It does not say, "Whoever has the right doctrine...." Jesus said, "I am the door. If anyone enters by Me, he will be saved, and will go in and out and find pasture." John 10:9.

Therefore, we look to Christ Jesus alone for our salvation. "In Him we live and move and have our being." Acts 17:28.

It is never a matter of our being saved by "in *what* we believe." It has always and only been a matter of our being saved by "in *whom* we believe."

May we walk together in love and unity knowing that regardless of our differences in belief, we are still one in Spirit. We are still sons of God who believe in Jesus Christ and obey His Holy Spirit.

Perhaps we will never find common ground in *what* we believe, but we can stand the ground on "in *whom* we believe."

33

SETTING THE TONE IN THE HOME

God the Father wrote a symphony and called it Family. Music, flowing down from heaven from the depths of His heart! Beautiful. Harmonious. Varying movements, crescendos and diminuendos.

Father God inspired this symphony. Jesus scored the music. The Holy Spirit conducts the orchestra. We are the instruments of various kinds: woodwinds, brass, percussion, and strings. We are as different as can be from each other; yet, together we make the music happen. We are the Family—a righteous family personified as an orchestra playing God's symphony!

The husband and dad of each godly household is the oboe in this orchestra—not all that celebrated, but his importance is distinct. He not only sounds the note by which all the other family members tune their instruments, but more importantly, he sets the tone for the home.

If the life he lives is off key, he will sound an irksome tone—not one from heaven. He will clash with the conductor and His music, and will throw the whole family into discord. The symphony cannot be performed. How important then is it that he sounds a pure note?

"Husbands, love your wives, just as Christ also loved the church (His assembly of called-out-ones His Bride), and gave Himself for her." Ephesians 5:25. "Husbands, love your wives, and do not be bitter toward them." Colossians 3:19. "Fathers, do not provoke your children, lest they become discouraged." Colossians 3:21.

If Dad's tuning note is true and any member of the family fails to tune the instrument of who they are to his, they will be in discord. Even when all others are in tune, the one who is out of tune throws the symphony into discord. "A little leaven leavens the whole lump." Galatians 5:9.

How beautiful is the sound of those who stay in tune with the music that flows from Father's heart. "Wives, submit to your own husbands, as to the Lord." Ephesians 5:22. "Children, obey your parents in all things: for this is well pleasing to the Lord." Colossians 3:20.

The Dad of the home does more than sound the pitch from which all others tune their instruments. He sets the tone for the home. Playing the right note is necessary, but there is more to the music. We can be in tune to the uniform pitch and still lack tone. Tone has to do with the quality of the note. He determines the quality of the music being played in his household.

Is it a warm, safe, compassionate, encouraging, and heartfelt tone? Is it one of peace or anger, comfort or fear, self-giving or self-centeredness, sharing or demanding, safety or danger, hope or despair, encouragement or disheartenment, criticism or compliments, instruction or blaming, laughter or grief, happiness or depression, godly discipline or lawlessness, unity or chaos, faith or fear, righteousness or sin, strength or weakness, guidance or control, nourishment or toxicity, caring or abusiveness? Is it a Holy Spirit atmosphere or demonic? It will be one or the other.

34

LOVE IS A CHOICE

Have you ever thought of God as a living personality with feelings? A quick glance through the scriptures reveals that God is love, patient, kind, good, merciful, faithful, generous, and forgiving. He also expresses emotions such as wrath, jealousy, and anger.

Regardless of the emotion, one thing is absolute. God is altogether just and good. He cannot be or do otherwise. Even in His wrath, He is just. He is, after all, God. He is the Creator. "Our God is in heaven; He does whatever He pleases." Psalm 115:3.

Perhaps the most dominant characteristic of God's nature is love. God *is* love. He does not just show love now and then. He *is* love by His very nature. He wants us to know, receive, and experience His love.

God's love is unconditional and sacrificial. Nothing can dissuade Him from loving us. "God so loved the world that He gave His only begotten Son, that whoever believes in Him should not perish, but have everlasting life." John 3:16.

That God's love is unconditional is evidenced in the fact

that "while we were yet sinners, Christ died for us." Romans 5:8. Regardless of our actions, He still loves us just as the father of the prodigal (wasteful) son never ceased to love him. Luke 15:11-31.

Nevertheless, love is a choice. It has to be. If it were not a choice, it would not be love. We cannot force someone to love us. That would be suppression. I cannot imagine God wrestling us to the ground and tickling our ribs until we cry "uncle."

Love is a commitment and demands a heart response. In the Old Testament God commanded, "Hear, O Israel: The LORD our God, the LORD is one! You shall love the LORD your God with all your heart, with all your soul, and with all your strength." Deuteronomy 6:4-5. Jesus confirmed this as the first and greatest commandment. Mark 12:30.

God has given us incredible free will. We can choose Him or reject Him. He will not force Himself upon us. While nothing can keep God from loving us, we can sabotage that love by rejecting Him. We hinder ourselves from receiving His unconditional, sacrificial love. God does not condemn us. We condemn ourselves. "And this is the condemnation, that the light has come into the world, and men loved darkness rather than light, because their deeds were evil." John 3:19. We can arrogantly get in God's face and defy Him. We can incur His wrath. And He can, if He so chooses, wipe us off the face of the earth. He is God.

Choosing God is all about choosing His love as profoundly demonstrated through the sacrifice of His Son, Jesus Christ. We respond to His love with love. We passionately love Him because He first loved us. Moreover, because of our love, we will keep His commandments. John 14:15.

There is "hell to pay" if we reject the love of God and heaven to gain if we accept.

Once we taste the goodness of His love, we take on His kind of love. Therefore, we demonstrate the love of God by the love we have toward our neighbors. Jesus commanded that we love one another as He has loved us. John 15:12. Love for one another is how the world will know that we are His disciples. John 13:35.

I strongly recommend that you respond to God's love at all cost to yourself. You get to choose how it will be.

35

OLD DOGS AND NEW TRICKS

Surely you have heard, "You can't teach an old dog new tricks." Consider this. You cannot teach new-creature ways to old-creature humans.

Paul, the apostle, writing to the believers in Corinth wrote, "Therefore, if anyone be in Christ, he is a new creation." (The King James Bible translates this word "creature"). 2 Corinthians 5:17a.

If there is such a thing as a "new creature," there has to have been an "old creature." Paul continued to proclaim that "Old things have passed away; behold, all things have become new." 2 Corinthians 5:17b. The context for "all things" is anyone in Christ.

Here, then, is the difference between the old creature and the new creature. The old creature is one of sin and death. The new creature is one of righteousness and life. Jesus plainly told Nicodemus, "You must be born again." New creature behavior cannot come forth out of an old creature nature. Something fundamentally has to change. Paul wrote, "I have been crucified with Christ; it is no longer I who live, but Christ lives in me; and the life which I now live in the flesh I live by faith in the Son of God, who loved me and gave Himself for me." Galatians 2:20.

There are many good people in the world who live a good Christian life and that is far better than the alternative. However, Paul is talking about living the exchanged life—no longer we who live, but Christ who lives in us.

We might manage to live a virtuous Christian life in our own strength, but that is outward behavior. We can clean the outside of the cup, but the inside will still be dirty. On the other hand, if we clean the inside of the cup, the outside will automatically get cleaned. Jesus said that in so many words in Matthew 23:25-26.

We were never expected to perfect ourselves. How can the dead raise itself up? Something greater than ourselves has to intervene and do for us what we could not do for ourselves. Paul explained, "But God, who is rich in mercy, because of His great love with which He loved us, even when we were dead in trespasses, made us alive together with Christ, and raised us up together, and made us sit together in the heavenly places in Christ Jesus, that in the ages to come He might show the exceeding riches of His grace in His kindness toward us in Christ Jesus. *For by grace you have been saved through faith, and that not of yourselves; it is the gift of God, not of works, lest anyone should boast.* For we are His workmanship, created in Christ Jesus for good works, which God prepared beforehand that we should walk in them." Ephesians 2:4-10 (italics mine).

We may not be able to teach old dogs new tricks; nevertheless, young or old, one thing remains certain for us humans: What we are on the inside will eventually drive what we do on the outside. Outside behavior will never change the inside nature. Rather, the inside nature changes the outside behavior.

Believe it or not, we really do need to be born again from on high by the power of the Holy Spirit. We really do need to be made new creatures in Christ Jesus, our Lord. We are never too old to be changed by the redeeming work of Christ. And that's the gospel truth!

36

FOLLOWING JESUS

Doris was thankful to have her job at the local post office. Her enthusiasm, however, was elsewhere. "I would rather be out on the street telling others about Jesus," she confided.

"What would you say to them?" I asked.

"I would ask them if they were saved, or if they were assured they would go to heaven when they died."

I responded by suggesting a different approach. "What if you went up to someone and asked, 'Have you decided yet?' They, no doubt, would look puzzled and ask, 'Decided what?' 'Have you decided to deny yourself, take up your cross, to follow Jesus?'"

Doris was certain. "They wouldn't know what I was talking about."

"Exactly," I answered. "That has not been preached."

We understand what it means to perform various religious rituals and duties. Some individuals may even make great sacrifices in the mission field or may do various charitable works, but the people who know what it means to follow Jesus in this manner are fewer in number. Yet, is that not the call of the Master? Jesus said to His disciples, "If any one desires to come after Me, let him deny himself, and take up his cross, and follow Me." Matthew 16:24.

Among the few who preach this call to follow Jesus are those who often put the emphasis upon the "deny self" part. Self, as meant in this context, is that sinful flesh nature of fallen man. "We've got to crucify the flesh," they contend. Consequently, they suffer repeated spiritual defeat. Why? Because they cannot crucify themselves!

Moreover, they miss the point. They actually engage in self-centeredness when they focus on trying to deny Self. That will not work. It works the other way around. *The choice to follow Jesus is the cross that denies self.*

Simon Peter and his brother Andrew were fishermen by trade and were casting their net into the sea when this stranger from Galilee strolled by and called them out. "Follow Me, and I will make you fishers of men." They straightway left their nets and followed Jesus. Matthew 4:18-20. Imagine that!

Sure, they denied themselves and took up their crosses to follow Jesus. But they did not spend years trying to beat their sinful flesh to death. They did not consider the weight of sin on their backs. No! They did first things first. They dropped their nets, left their boat floating by the shore, and took off after this man whose call to "follow Me" penetrated their hearts.

We are called to follow Jesus. Sure, there will be choices to make and a price to pay. Precious believers in troubled parts of the world today are being persecuted, violated, and killed every day because of their unrelenting choice to follow Jesus. Persecution and martyrdom is their cross.

Nevertheless, following Jesus does not follow the denial of self. Denying self follows following Jesus. (Read it again, slowly). The cross we bear is not the act of denying self. The cross we bear is the decision to follow Jesus.

Self-flagellation is worthless navel-gazing condemnation. The time one spends trying to deny his flesh is time wasted from following Jesus.

Following Jesus is a decision from deep within our spirits. It is a matter of agreeing with the Spirit of Christ, testifying that we are no longer our own. 1 Corinthians 6:19. We have been bought with a price. 1 Corinthians 7:23. We belong to Jesus. He can do with us as He pleases. We surrender and He takes it from there.

37

AMERICA BLESS GOD

Surely you have seen them peppered about, those bumper stickers and marquees, pleading, "God Bless America." But why, we might ask, would God bless America (or any other nation for that matter) when growing numbers of its citizens make a mockery of Him, even shaking their fist in His face? We are more likely to bow the knee to what is "politically correct" than to honor the heart of God.

If we want to honor God's heart, we have no further to look than to Deuteronomy 28. Read it and see for yourself. There are two parts with conditions to this narrative. In the first part, God told of all the ways in which He would bless Israel "if".... There is always that agonizing, "if." If they diligently obeyed His voice and carefully observed His commandments. All these blessings not only would come upon them, but they would overtake them.

He promised to bless them in the city and in the country, to bless the fruit of their body, the produce of the ground, their herds, their basket and kneading bowl, and their coming in and going out. He promised to cause their enemies to be defeated and flee. They will come in one way and flee before them seven ways. He promised to command the blessing on their storehouses and bless all to which they set their hands to do. Can you imagine God commanding His blessing upon you? Even overtaking you?

"But!" There is always that agonizing, "But!" It begins the second part of this passage of scripture. God said, "But, it shall come to pass, if you do not obey the voice of the Lord your God, to observe carefully all His commandments and His statutes which I command you today, that all these curses will come upon you and overtake you." The blessings of obedience are reversed in the acts of disobedience. The list of curses is much longer than the list of blessings. (The passage is too long to quote for this column. You really should read it. It is profound.)

We simply cannot make God up to be what we want Him to be and think He is okay with that. Malachi 3:6 reads, "For I am the LORD, I do not change." Yet, that is what we have done in the courts of our land, in our personal lives, and in many pulpits. We want God to bless America while we live as we please. When He does not bless our stuff, we huff and puff. We get mad at Him and assert, "God is dead."

Jesus, who is the summation of all that God requires of us, proclaimed, "Seek first the Kingdom of God and His righteousness and all of these things shall be added to you." Matthew 6:33. We need only to chase after God. "He is a rewarder of those who diligently seek Him." Hebrews 11:6.

2 Chronicles 7:14 is still relevant. "if My people who are called by My name will humble themselves, and pray and seek My face, and turn from their wicked ways, then I will hear from heaven, and will forgive their sin and heal their land."

Well then! We might want to reverse the words on our bumper stickers. Rather than pleading, "God Bless America," we might want to plead "America Bless God." Bless Him by pursuing Him—His Kingdom and His righteousness. We might just find out how miraculously God will involve Himself in our lives and in our nation—America or otherwise.

38

GIVE THANKS
WITH A GRATEFUL HEART

Our dear friend was as dedicated a believer in and follower of Jesus Christ as anyone I had met in my
Christian experience. He, his wife, and numerous others of
like mind met regularly in each other's homes. It was often
"wall to wall" Jesus talk.

My wife and I were introduced to this cluster of believers
after moving into their community years ago. We ate with
this friend and his wife often and I noticed he never initiated
"saying a blessing" before our meals. I asked him about that.
"A while back," he explained, "a bunch of us were together
sitting around sharing Jesus. It came time to eat and we
stopped to say the blessing. It was as if we took a break from
being in His presence to say this blessing. It felt 'religious' to
us so we stopped saying it. We just continued on in His fellowship." He added rhetorically, "Do we give thanks when
we fill our cars up with gas?"

I understood, though it took me a while to get past the
"religious" part of saying a rote blessing before a meal. Since

then, I am not ritualistic about saying the blessing. Whether I voice something out loud or not does not make me any more or less grateful.

Nevertheless, I began to think. "Well, no, I do not give thanks when I fill my car tank with gas, but that is not a bad idea." So I reasoned, instead of not giving thanks for food because I did not give thanks for gas in my car, why not give thanks for both the food and the gas, and everything else for that matter.

This whole discussion made me far more grateful of all that we owe to the goodness of God. After all, "Every good gift and every perfect gift is from above, and comes down from the Father of lights, with whom there is no variation or shadow of turning." James 1:17.

I am acutely aware of the poverty in our own back yard and believe we must do what we can to alleviate it. Nevertheless, so many of us who live in America, compared to others, are blessed beyond measure.

Our gratitude is not just for food. Oh, my! Look in our closets, our houses, our vehicles, and our rented storage units to accommodate the stuff we do not have room for in our houses.

My wife and I had to replace our refrigerator recently and I thought, "What a blessing to have such a problem." That we had the resources to replace it was a blessing. We had to borrow someone's portable refrigerator until the new refrigerator arrived. Becky Jane Newbold's editorial in the September 2014 issue of *Validity* aptly labeled these as, "First world problems."

Our gratitude toward God ought not be driven by our circumstances. Rather, to echo Paul, the apostle, let us be content in whatsoever state we find ourselves.

We need not feel guilty for God's blessings in our lives, we just need to make sure we are not taking God for granted or, worse yet, boast in ourselves that we have "pulled ourselves up by our own boot straps."

We want to continually give thanks to God with a grateful heart for all that He has done for us.

"Thank you Father not only for our daily bread, but for all of our creature comforts. Most especially, we praise you for so great a salvation as we have in your Son, Jesus Christ."

39

A HUG FROM JESUS

Two thousand years ago or so a child was born in Bethlehem whose name was Jesus (Yeshua, in Hebrew). He was called the Son of God. He was both fully God and fully man having been born of the Virgin Mary and conceived by the Holy Sprit.

The opening words in John's gospel reads, "In the beginning was the Word, and the Word was with God, and the Word was God. He was in the beginning with God. All things were made through Him, and without Him nothing was made that was made." John 1:1-3. John proclaimed that "the Word was God."

Paul, the apostle, described Christ Jesus this way. He, "being in the form of God, did not consider it robbery to be equal with God, but made Himself of no reputation, taking the form of a bondservant, and coming in the likeness of men." Philippians 2:5-7.

As He grew, He increased in wisdom and stature, and in favor with God and men. Luke 2:52. He died on the cross, was buried, rose the third day, ascended into heaven and sits on the right hand of God, the Father.

During His earthly ministry, Jesus told a Pharisee named Nicodemus that he had to be "born again." John 3. We learn from Galatians 3:26 and 4:6 that when we are born again by grace through faith we become the sons of God.

Jesus was first born into the world. Then, He is birthed in us when we are born again from on high by the Holy Spirit. The same Holy Spirit that birthed Him, re-birthed us. The new birth works both ways. He is born into us and we are born into Him. Jesus claimed that we are in Him and He is in us just as He is in the Father. John 14:20.

Awesome! But do not ask me how this works. We take it by faith and we come to know it is true because we find Him working in and through us. "The Spirit Himself bears witness with our spirit that we are children (sons) of God." Romans 8:16. We just know!

Additionally, "we all, with unveiled face, beholding as in a mirror the glory of the Lord, are being transformed into the same image from glory to glory, just as by the Spirit of the Lord." 2 Corinthians 3:18.

Think about the numerous times we go through a checkout lane. How likely are we to give much thought that, as we go, we carry within us the very presence of the Almighty. Who can say what influence He may be having on others through us? We may need to tie a little ribbon on our thumb to remind us.

Likewise, we are unlikely to give thought to the places and conditions into which we may drag Him. We trudge through life with an awareness of our own weaknesses and strengths, but with little awareness of His divine presence and power within us. If, indeed Christ is in us, we are like little arks of His covenant, carrying about His Presence wherever we go.

Let us live with that glorious awareness that He is in us and we are in Him! Ambassadors! May our words and actions be those of the living Christ within us.

If indeed Christ is in you, the next time you give someone as simple a thing as a righteous hug, it will not just be you hugging. That person will get a loving hug from Jesus as well.

40

I LOVE KNOWING...

We all have our favorite verses of scripture. I particularly love those that tell me who I am in Christ and who He is in me.

I love knowing that I have been born again and have eternal life, because I believe in God's only begotten Son, Jesus Christ. John 3:16. I love knowing that!

I love knowing I have been redeemed by the blood of the Lamb—Jesus Christ (Revelation 5:9), who, while I was yet a sinner, died for me. Romans 5:8.

I love knowing I have been saved by grace through faith and that it was a free gift from God and not of my own works lest I should boast. Ephesians 2:8-9.

I love knowing I am His workmanship, created in Christ Jesus unto good works that God ordained before hand that I should walk in them. Ephesians 2:10.

I love knowing I have been buried with Him through baptism into death, and as Christ was raised from the dead by the glory of the Father, I am able to walk in newness of life. Romans 6:4.

I love knowing I have been crucified with Christ; it is no longer I who live, but Christ lives in me; and the life that I now live in the flesh I live by faith in the Son of God, who loved me and gave Himself for me. Galatians 2:20.

I love knowing I am no longer my own. I have been bought with a price. 1 Corinthians 6:19-20. The Lord can do with me as He wills.

I love knowing in Christ Jesus I live and move and have my being because I am His offspring. Acts 17:28.

I love knowing that He has begun a good work in me and He will complete it until the day of Jesus Christ. Philippians 1:6.

I love knowing all things work together for good to those who love God, those who are the called according to His purpose. Romans 8:28.

I love knowing Christ in Me is my hope of glory. Colossians 1:27.

I love knowing I am in Jesus and He is in me, just as He is in the Father and the Father is in Him. John 17:20-23.

I love knowing God is working in me what is well pleasing in His sight, through Jesus Christ. Hebrews 13:21.

I love knowing, one day, when I see Him as He is, I will be like Him. 1 John 3:2.

I love knowing, even while I am still in the world, I am as He is. 1 John 4:17.

I love knowing the manner of love the Father has bestowed upon me was such, that He would call me a son of God. 1 John 3:1.

I love knowing this is not just about me. The "I" is "we."

Put yourself in these scriptures. They apply to all who have in fact accepted Jesus Christ as their Lord. I love knowing that about us, don't you?

10665814R20070

Made in the USA
Monee, IL
01 September 2019